Angels
BESIDE
YOU

Shawn, Erin, Avery, Carter

Page 69

I hope you enjoy the
story. Paul W Fouts

OTHER BOOKS AND AUDIO BOOKS

BY JUDY C. OLSEN

Beyond the Horizon

Angels Round About: True Stories of the Lord's Tender Mercies

Angels to Bear You up: True Stories of the Lord's Tender Mercies

Angels Watching Over You: True Stories of the Lord's Tender Mercies

Angels Near and Far, Audio book on CD

Angels Watching Over You, Audio book on CD

Angels
BESIDE
YOU

True Stories
of the Lord's
Tender Mercies

Covenant Communications, Inc.

To my parents, who taught me correct principles

ACKNOWLEDGMENTS

I wish to thank all the people who have contributed to this volume. Each of them has offered a spiritual insight learned through facing hard challenges, offering meaningful prayer, or enduring difficult trials that have brought them ever closer to God. We too are strengthened as we read of their struggles and faith to overcome.

I also want to thank the editorial, artistic, and marketing staff at Covenant for their hard work and help in publishing this book.

$\mathcal{I}$NTRODUCTION

Everyone faces adversity in life. This is the Lord's program for our growth and development. With each challenge—and we will all have many—we learn to cope, understand, and trust, as well as exercise greater faith in our Heavenly Father. As challenges and difficulties present themselves, the Lord extends to us the remarkable invitation to come unto Him for guidance, peace, help, and sometimes miracles.

In the stories found in this fourth volume of True Stories of the Lord's Tender Mercies, we read about many different kinds of struggles. Some people feel the love of God as they are guided through challenging times. Others learn to trust in Him as they keep the commandments. And still others feel Heavenly Father's love when they receive help in solving problems. In each case, faith and prayers open spiritual doors for obtaining help beyond the person's capacity. Obtaining such help is a fulfillment of the Lord's promises found in Doctrine and Covenants 24:8: "Be patient in afflictions, for thou shalt have many; but endure them, for, lo, I am with thee, even unto the end of thy days."

He is indeed there for us too.

—Judy Olsen

CONTENTS

SECTION III: WE FEEL HIS LOVE AS WE ARE GUIDED IN HOW TO SOLVE
OUR PROBLEMS

WE FEEL HIS LOVE WHEN WE DEAL WITH UNEXPECTED CHALLENGES

To every thing there is a season. . . . A time to be born, and a time to die; . . . A time to kill, and a time to heal; a time to break down, and a time to build up.

—Ecclesiastes 3:1–3

NOT MY TIME TO DIE
By Dan Perkins

In 1979 my wife and I had been living in Sandy, Utah, for just over a year, and we had two young boys under two years of age. At the time, I drove a large semitruck for a living. I had contracted with a modular home company in Salt Lake City to transport and place their homes on new foundations. Modular homes were in demand at that time in many small towns in the Intermountain West, and I had lots of experience doing this kind of work and kept very busy.

Each house, built in a local factory, consisted of two or more sections. After loading these sections on large trailers, we would take them to their destinations. Once there, we would jack them up with heavy-duty jacks, then place heavy steel beams and rollers under them and across the foundation. Using winches, we carefully pulled the house sections into position. Finally, we would jack up one end of a house section at a time, remove the beams, and then lower the house onto the foundation.

Just before Thanksgiving, I was assigned to take a house to the southeast corner of Utah. I had been raised in the small town of Monticello, so I felt I was going home. I even still had family in the area.

It was a cold, winter Monday morning when we left Salt Lake City. Snow had fallen in places along the road overnight, and by the time we got to Monticello, it was too late to start placing the house.

Tuesday morning we got an early start. After jacking up the first half of the house and moving it to its final position, my helper, Tom, and I set our jacks on the snowy basement floor and, working from underneath the house, began the careful and delicate process of lifting the first house section a few inches to remove the beams and rollers in preparation to lower it onto the foundation.

Suddenly, I caught movement out of the corner of my eye. Shocked, I realized the house had started to tip off the jacks. This could *not* be happening! We were virtually trapped in the basement directly under the house section. In a panic, I turned to run and called out a warning to Tom just as the house came crashing down right on top of both of us.

I was pinned under a 20,000-pound house, and as blackness surrounded me, my last thought was *I'm going to die.* The next thing I recalled was that I was moving through darkness toward light just ahead of me. Then I passed through a veil into extreme light.

Everything was beautifully white and bright. People were standing in front of me only a short distance away. I saw my grandfather, who had died when I was in my early teens. He had been hit by a truck while riding a horse across a bridge. As a child, I had followed him around, ridden horses with him, and idealized him. There were other people with him, standing on a smooth surface, and I vaguely recall pillars and some indistinct landscape behind them. Grandpa looked different from what I remembered of him as an old man, but I recognized his younger-looking self immediately. In that moment, a feeling of peace, contentment, and joy washed over me.

Somewhere behind me, I heard my name called, so I turned and stepped back into darkness. The next thing I knew, I was looking up at the sky, lying on that cold, snowy basement floor in excruciating pain.

A man I had grown up with, who had become a paramedic, was calling my name. "Dan! Can you hear me?" (Later—much later—I told him he had literally called me back to my body.)

Eventually, I pieced together what happened moments after the house fell. A neighbor had seen the accident and called the emergency response crew, and a large group of people had gathered to try to save us. One worker on the site grabbed the jacks and lifted the timbers enough for the men to extricate me from under the house.

I went to the hospital, where they determined I had compression fractures in my back, a damaged right knee, and various other scrapes and bruises. I also learned that Tom, who had been trapped farther under the house, was barely alive. He never regained consciousness and passed away about a week later. The pain of his passing hurt deeply. I often agonized over what went wrong and how his death might have been prevented, but I will never completely understand what happened on that cold and snowy day. I was released from the hospital in time to get to Salt Lake City for his funeral.

As the months went by, my body slowly healed. I often thought of the moment when I stepped from darkness into light, but I never told anyone about it. I *couldn't* talk about it. Had I imagined it? What of my friend Tom? I felt guilty because I lived while he died. I sometimes woke up at night shaking and crying. I blamed myself for his death.

About fifteen years later, while I was talking to a close friend, Bill, I finally shared what had happened to me while I was trapped under the house. I then went home and, for the first time, told my patient and loving wife about it.

Later still, at a family gathering, I finally told my brother-in-law what I had experienced. He said, "Hold on. Everybody needs to hear this."

It was then, all those years later, that my family heard my story. Then my father asked, "Why didn't you tell us before now?"

I said I wasn't sure I could really explain it.

For the first time, we talked about it as a family, and I learned things I hadn't known about that day. Dad and my brother had been in Bluff, Utah, attending a business meeting. A Utah highway patrol officer had come into the room and told Dad about the accident—that I had been seriously hurt. Dad and my brother raced out of the meeting and sped north to Monticello, forty miles away. But as my brother was driving, he suddenly slowed down. Dad asked him why.

"Dan is all right," he said.

My father also told me the sheriff at the scene of the accident that day had jumped down into the basement and examined my body, then told the emergency crew I was dead and to *leave me be*. Thankfully, my EMT friend didn't listen and instead jumped down to try to revive me.

Once I shared my story, I found it easier to talk about it. One day about five years later, I was driving my semitruck across a back road in Central Oregon. I started to talk on the CB radio with a driver in the truck just in front of me. He asked me how I was doing, and I replied with the usual response I had given ever since the accident: "I'm just happy to be here!" I also mentioned that I was a member of the Church.

He told me he was also a member of the Church and asked me about my reply, so I told my story of that tragic day. He turned quiet for a few minutes, then he told me of his own near-death experience.

He and his friend, he explained, had been in a car that slid off the road into a ravine in the mountains above Pocatello, Idaho. His friend had died, but he had lived. He told me that he had left his body and watched as emergency personnel worked to save his life. And like me, he continued to hold on to a great deal of guilt that he had lived while his friend had died. Then he admitted that he had never told anyone what had happened when his spirit left his body. I was the first to hear his story.

We continued talking, and I told him he needed to share his story, to tell his mother, family, friends, and all who would listen. I felt that perhaps I had waited too long and had since learned that sharing brought relief, peace, and finally acceptance, even contentment, and that it had helped me let go of the guilt.

A small town came into sight, and my new friend said, "Stop up ahead, will you? I would like to meet you."

We pulled off the road, parked, and exited our trucks. We shook hands, and he said, "Hi, I'm Danny!"

Startled, I replied, "Hi, I'm also Danny!"

We visited a while, and again, I encouraged him to share his story.

We never met again, but I have always felt I was there that day to help Danny through something very similar to what I had gone through. I know I was on that back road at that time to help him.

Now when I look back on that day years ago when a house literally fell on me, I realize how close I came to dying. But for some reason, I was sent back to spend thirty-four more years with my loving wife, have two more sons for a total of four, and spend time with our eight grandchildren, whom we adore.

Because of the response of heroic people and the will of the Lord, I have had a good life. I'm grateful our Heavenly Father granted me these extra years so I could go home to my soul mate, my wife, to help raise my sons. I have had a great life with my family and have had a lot of fun.

As I have said ever since that day, "I'm just glad to be here!" In the book of Ecclesiastes, we read that there is a time to be born and a time to die. I'm grateful that my time to die was not on that day in 1979. I'm also very grateful that I've been given a time to heal.

Dan Perkins still lives in Sandy, Utah, with his wife. Two of their sons are married, and between them, they have eight children. Dan enjoys retirement and spending time with family and friends. He likes to camp, take river-rafting trips, and go four-wheeling. He also enjoys fishing and playing pool with friends. After two recent knee surgeries, he continues to reaffirm, "I'm just glad to be here!"

When thou art in tribulation, and all these things are come upon thee, even in the latter days, if thou turn to the Lord thy God, and shalt be obedient unto his voice; (For the Lord thy God is a merciful God;) he will not forsake thee.

—Deuteronomy 4:30–31

HOW WOULD I COPE?
By Linda Serra

Because of a buyout that had taken place with the company where I worked, I was under a lot of pressure. Day after day, things became more tense. Many disrespectful and offensive things happened, one of which was a targeting scam against dedicated workers in the company. We found ourselves having to defend each other from documentation that had been altered, setting individuals up for dismissal. Everyone felt the strain. Constant worry made interaction with coworkers increasingly difficult.

But I prayerfully approached each day with an attitude of gratitude and appreciation for those among my associates who, I hoped, stood by me. Still, it was hard to know who might be targeted next. I would go home at night knowing a restful sleep would be hard to find. Anxiety overwhelmed me, to say the least. One night I lay down, needing relief from the stress and tension that had taken over my body for so long. I was *so* exhausted. I don't know why, other than the fact that I was purely exhausted, but that night I fell into a much-needed deep sleep.

When I awoke in the morning, I couldn't see. I made my way to the bathroom. The light was on, yet I couldn't see. Thinking something had gotten into my eyes, I washed them. I *still* couldn't see anything. What was going on?

I told my husband. "Something is wrong. I need to go to the doctor."

My husband drove me to an InstaCare, and they sent me to an ophthalmologist. After a series of tests, the doctor told me that a combination of high blood pressure and stress had contributed to strokes in the optic nerves of my eyes. My diagnosis was 20/300. I was told I couldn't drive anymore, that I was legally blind, and that it was permanent. I broke down and began to sob. Later, they found my optic nerves to be the size of an infant's, which they said was *very* unusual. That might have been why the strokes had hit that area.

I couldn't imagine my life going forward the way I was. Of course, my job ended that day too. What was I going to do?

In those first days of living in darkness, I went home to be with my mother. Initially, I thought I was totally blind, but I soon realized the blindness I was experiencing was very manageable. I had *some* sight. Nevertheless, I felt I had a right to feel miserable. I tried living with misery for a while, but it wasn't in my character to stay that way.

I attended church soon after and met an old friend there. Her husband offered to give me a priesthood blessing, and after he did, he told me he had felt impressed that he should *not* tell me my sight would be restored. Rather, this was a condition I was *expected to endure well*. During the blessing, I also strongly felt a witness of the Spirit confirming this very counsel. Immediately, my attitude changed to accept *whatever* happened. I returned home to begin the process of learning how to cope.

My neighbor had a relative associated with the state's School for the Blind and Visually Impaired. He visited me and soon set wheels in motion to help me get my life put together again. I attended classes and learned to adjust to my new disability. I learned how to cook and clean with new consideration for my lack of vision. I learned beginning Braille and how to use a computer with the assistance of programs specifically developed for eye impairment. They taught me how to use a cane for identification of obstacles in my path and for sure footing in getting around.

What a world I was now experiencing! Recognizing people I knew became more difficult, and it was painful to realize some people were uncomfortable with disabilities and shied away from acceptance. As the complications at home mounted, problems arose in our marriage, and after thirty-four years together, my husband left. God became my closest friend and confidant.

At the school, I met many people adjusting, as I was, to many degrees of vision loss. I became fascinated with them and their stories. As we each selected our individual pathway for moving forward, we formed close bonds. Watching those around me gave me strength and initiative to realize I had a purpose to fulfill. I could be an example and help others understand issues pertaining to blindness.

Opportunities for speaking and interacting with those who had the ability to help and understand others with disabilities became one of my focuses. Since my blindness began, I've sat on many boards and councils, including our state advisory committee for educational input on disability issues. I've worked with the legislature to promote efforts that will alleviate deficiencies in the systems that serve the disabled. I have worked 24/7 on anything I've thought would make a difference, and I continue to be astonished at the accomplishments of so many people with disabilities.

Of course, God has been my anchor and companion throughout this long journey. I continue to have good days and bad days, but for the most part, the comforting assurance from the words of the priesthood blessing I received in those first weeks has kept me steady. This is a challenge I am expected to bear well.

I am grateful for good friends and good neighbors and helpful ward members. They have made an enormous difference. The problems that plagued my former workplace eventually caught up with them, and the company went out of business. As hard as those days were, I felt the Lord watching over me at every difficult turn. Today I am especially grateful to my Father in Heaven, who has helped me and guided my every step since.

Linda Serra, a convert to the Church, lives in Bountiful, Utah. She has two children and two grandchildren, three sisters, and a brother. She is active in Church and community programs and in giving service. She loves the Lord and prays daily to do what is right and keep the commandments. "The Lord is my Shepherd," she says, "and I walk daily with my hand in His."

Behold my Spirit is upon you, wherefore all thy words will I justify; and the mountains shall flee before you, and the rivers shall turn from their course; and thou shalt abide in me, and I in you; therefore walk with me.

—*Moses 6:34*

ANGELS IN HEAVEN AND ON EARTH

By Shelise Santore-Tovar

Sometime after I married and started a family, I prayed while driving my minivan: *Heavenly Father, help me become a better person. Let me be the sacrifice so I can have righteous children.* In light of the life-altering events that were to come, I believe God answered that prayer.

In 2008 I went from being a very active mom to a woman whose health spiraled into a steep decline. No doctor could figure out what was behind my steady slide into poor health. In a priesthood blessing, I was told that I would find out what was wrong and that I would have angels in heaven and on earth to lift me through my trial.

I was attending college, teaching preschool, working out and working part-time at a gym, and raising three children. However, my husband, Art, and I did not have health insurance. I became an A student who could no longer lift my head off the desk. I felt so tired that I would often fall asleep just driving the few minutes to school. I knew I was dying, and I even told my visiting teacher I had written a note, which I kept in my purse, just in case something terrible happened while I was at school.

My ward Relief Society sisters stepped in to offer help. After months of uncertainty, doctors finally discovered what was going on. A crack had developed in the exhaust manifold of my minivan. Unknown to us, exhaust had been spilling into my air conditioning/heating vents *for over fourteen months.* My car had been slowing killing me, and I now have permanent brain damage from carbon monoxide poisoning.

The first time I went into the hospital for treatment, I was scared. I had always been so healthy! In high school, I participated in track, cross country, dance, and basketball. This was such new territory for me. I didn't know what to expect. And because my husband had to care for our children at home and return to work the next day, he, after checking me in, left me alone at the hospital and drove the hour back to our house. Feeling forlorn and frightened, I sought comfort in prayer. As I lay there, a voice inside me quietly brought peace: *You are not alone. God is with you. He loves you. You are never alone.*

Then I started having trouble breathing. At first, I could breathe out but not in. Soon I could do neither. I had stopped breathing. The thought crossed my mind to push the call button, which I managed to do, and a nurse quickly appeared and coached me as he put an oxygen mask on my face. Frightened that I was dying, I begged the Lord for my life. *Please, Lord, I have a husband and children, and they are not here. Please don't take me now.* Suddenly, I could breathe again. I was so excited.

"You saved my life," I told the nurse.

They kept me on oxygen for two days. As the problem became better understood, the doctors sent me to undergo hyperbaric-chamber treatments for forty days. We had to drive almost two hours to San Diego for the therapy. At first, Art was unavailable to help me, so my mother came out to be with me the first week; then the Relief Society sisters stepped in and drove me daily to the brain injury center for treatment. The days ran together, dragging on and on, and I thought this stage of treatment would never end. It was a daily fight just to keep myself going.

The next stage of treatment involved thirty days of intensive cognitive, physical, speech, occupational, and neuropsychology therapy at the Casa Colina treatment center. These therapies, which I had never heard of before, now took up my entire day, not to mention the Casa Colina center was an hour-and-a-half drive from home.

About this time, Art lost his job. As hard as that was, it was also a blessing for me. He began driving me every day and waiting for me until my treatments were finished. My health problems took over our lives. I began to live two separate lives: one at the Casa Colina treatment center during the day and one at home in the late evening trying to act normal for my husband and children. It was a daily struggle.

While at the center, I worked hard, doing hours of therapy. In the meantime, my husband homeschooled our daughter in the hospital library and played soccer with her outside. At noon Art would check me out for lunch, and we would eat at the hospital cafeteria together. I lived for those moments of normalcy with my daughter and husband and thought often of my two older teen boys, who were at school all day. At four o'clock, my husband would sign me out, and then we would make the long drive home in traffic. We did this every day for thirty days.

During lunch at the center, I often looked around at the other patients undergoing therapies, and one day I realized I was one of them. *Look at all of us*, I thought. *How did we all get here? We are all God's children with a purpose. Some of us have had our minds fail us, others our bodies. Some of us have had both fail us. We are all here for different reasons. We all have families, a life beyond here. Our disabilities scare others. They look at us and think*, What happened to them? Could it happen to me? Yes! *It can happen to anyone at any time.*

I have had to learn to take it one day at a time. Over the last few years, my kids have helped me and gone with me to many outpatient therapies. In the beginning, it was an adjustment for all of us. Before I was able to obtain my own wheelchair, my boys or husband would carry me. Once, my family even put me in a shopping cart, which my husband pushed while the kids pushed the food cart. A child sitting in a passing shopping cart stared at me and asked, "Why is that mommy in the shopping cart?" His mother, embarrassed, hurried him quickly away and said sometimes mommies can ride in the carts too. We all got a good laugh at that one.

Thankfully, I do not ride in shopping carts anymore. Now I have a sparkly girly wheelchair that glows in the dark. But acceptance came slowly, and I am still working on it. One day I removed all the photos of the old me from off the walls of our home. I just couldn't look at them anymore—they had become painful reminders of how athletic I had once been and my dreams of what I hoped one day to achieve.

I am not the same person I was before, but I am starting to like the new me.

I am finally accepting who I am now—a woman, wife, and mother with a permanent disability. But I am also so much more. I have learned to be more empathetic to others. I have an understanding that God gives us our breath of life. And I can finally feel comfortable taking photos of who I am: I am ready to share the new me with the world. With this acceptance, the day finally came when I was able to put back all the photos of the former me, along with new ones of who I am now.

Some of the things I thought were important before are not so important now. Going through this trial has given me a new perspective on life. I still enjoy some of the same things I did before, like getting flowers, watching romantic movies, and eating chocolate, and I still have weak moments, but we get through them together as a family.

I am so grateful that despite my many outward changes, my wonderful husband treats me the same. He sees me as *me*. He respects me and does not look down on me or make me feel small or stupid or childish because of the changes that occurred in my mind and body. I like to remember who the real me is, the whole and loving spirit who presently resides in a less-than-perfect body—the healthy, happy, fun, busy, loving person who once lived for and served others. On some good days, I see a glimpse of my old self, but as my brain tires, I lose more function. Those glimpses soon fade, and I am reminded of my new reality.

Art now works as a deputy sheriff, and I finally have insurance, a neurologist, and medication that helps. Because of the lack of oxygen to my brain, muscles, and every part of my body, I suffer not only from acquired brain injury but also from dystonia and chorea (involuntary muscle movements). Not one day is like the other: I experience a roller coaster of good and bad days. I never know what each day might bring. That is how neurological problems are.

I thank the Lord for being patient with all my emotions, confusion, frustration, and struggles over these last years. And I am very thankful for the gospel, which has provided a true foundation of beliefs and support to carry me through this trial. Because I can finally talk about it, I feel a weight lifted off my shoulders. I'm finding new friends who also have brain damage and similar health struggles, and I've become more understanding, developed many coping skills, and set goals to help me progress.

Perhaps you are also stuck in your own experience right now and are trying to heal. If you are someone with health struggles, please get to know the new you and love yourself for who you are now. It takes time, but when you embrace your life as it must be for now, you will see how many wonderful opportunities you still have. Just look around. God has a path, a plan, and patience for you.

Our choices are daily, and what we accomplish is up to us. I thank the Lord for the moments He has blessed me with to be with my children, husband, and other people who have become dear to me. Perhaps I can touch their lives as they have mine.

I sometimes think back to the prayer I uttered so long ago: *Heavenly Father, help me become a better person. Let me be the sacrifice so I can have righteous children.* I know the Lord has held my hand through some very hard days, and He truly has become my best friend through pain, sadness, and discouragement. He lifts me when I cannot lift myself and sometimes sends others to lift me also. I know He smiles down on me. I *have* become a better person, and our children—a rewarding work still in progress—have seen the hand of God in our lives. This trial has strengthened our faith and brought us closer as a family.

Shelise Santore-Tovar is a mother of three who loves nature. She and Art, her celestial companion, have been married for eighteen years. Shelise has held many callings in the Church, including teaching in Relief Society and working in a Relief Society presidency. She is going back to college for the first time since her brain injury in 2008. The couple recently bought a new house, and Shelise loves decorating it and making it into a comfortable family home. She also enjoys doing temple work and genealogy research. Sunday is her favorite day of the week because she feels spiritually fed at church and has many opportunities to bear her testimony.

Note: Shelise has seen gradual improvement. However, her story came to me through many e-mails, a portion at a time. I asked questions, and she answered them. Slowly, working together, we documented her story for this book. —Judy Olsen

Thou knowest the greatness of God; and he shall consecrate thine afflictions for thy gain.

—2 Nephi 2:2

THE BROKEN PIECE
By Ingrid Sanabria

On July 22, 2013, I became increasingly worried about my back pain, a condition that had bothered me on and off for over two years. I had previously experienced two especially painful episodes of back pain that had left me unable to move for two days, so on that day, when the pain started radiating down my leg, I became very concerned.

The physical therapy I had started a couple months earlier and all the gains I had made seemed to be erased. I quickly set an appointment to see my doctor. Two weeks later, I had an MRI, and the doctor concluded that the pain was due to a herniated disk. She recommended a steroid injection directly into the spine, which would take the pain away so I could continue physical therapy. I agreed to have the injection.

While I waited for the appointed day one week later, the pain in my back continued to increase daily. On the injection day, I was told the medicine could take up to two weeks to take full effect in reducing the pain, so I had to be patient. I had no other choice.

One week passed, and the pain only slightly decreased. I constantly prayed to Heavenly Father, asking Him to *please* take away the pain. Every morning I got out of bed with the hope that the pain would be less. One special night, I knelt, even though it was painful to do so, and I cried to the Lord, begging for healing. I said, "I want to serve Thee, to go out and do the things Thou needest me to do. I want to be an instrument in Thy hands."

I paused, and a clear thought came to my mind: *I don't want you to be the instrument in my hands. This time I need you to be the broken piece.* That thought sank into my heart. The *broken* piece? A feeling of

comfort and peace washed over me, and I knew God knew what I was
going through and that there was a reason for it.

At the same time, I was a bit sad and worried about what was going
to happen, how much longer I was going to be in pain, and just how
much it was going to hurt. I was grateful to friends who offered words
of comfort, encouragement, and support. I told myself, *Just keep going
and doing what the Lord wants you to do.*

After that night, there was no improvement. Finally, the day of my
two-week follow-up appointment arrived. Because the medicine had
not taken away the pain, the doctor recommended that I continue to
have more injections until I got better. When I asked how many that
might be, she told me she was not sure. The other option would be to
have surgery, which the doctor did not recommend. I left her office
disappointed, not knowing exactly what to do.

While researching back surgery, I came across a less invasive laser
surgical procedure that seemed promising. Looking back, I believe the
Spirit guided my husband and me to this other option. We decided I
should go ahead with the laser surgery.

It took time to set up the appointment for the procedure. Meanwhile,
my pain levels continued to increase daily. I had to stop working. The
pain was so strong that performing the most minimal task became an
excruciating experience; even sleeping seemed impossible. Every day I
had to remember to endure well. I would say to myself, *The Lord wants
me to be a broken piece.*

I felt like I was doing a great job at it! I knew my family and friends
were praying for me and thinking of me. Their visits, phone calls, and
support strengthened me.

Sleepless nights passed, and the days seemed so long! One morning,
almost a week before the procedure, I came upon the following verse in
the Book of Mormon: "I will also ease the burdens which are put upon
your shoulders, that even you cannot feel them upon your *backs* . . .
and this will I do that ye may *stand* as witnesses for me hereafter, and
that ye may know of a surety that I, the Lord God, do visit my people
in their afflictions" (Mosiah 24:14, emphasis added). I thought, *So . . .
one day I won't feel the burden in my back, and I will stand up, right?*

Once again I felt the love of God, that He was talking to me, but
this time I felt I was going to heal and be able to stand once more,
literally without pain, as a witness of the tender mercies of the Lord.

We met with the doctor in Phoenix, Arizona, for the first time on September 18. He explained what he was going to do and said it would take time for the pain to go away. He snapped his fingers and said, "I wish it could disappear just like that."

I thought, *Oh no! How much longer will I be in pain?*

He said it could take months, and then he continued to describe the whole procedure. I listened as my husband asked questions.

The next day my husband gave me a blessing. The part I remember best is that I was told I needed to be patient. I felt comforted and knew everything was going to be okay.

We arrived at the clinic and found a whole team of caring professionals, both doctors and nurses, waiting for us. I felt such peace that I thought angels must be surrounding me as I was put to sleep.

When I woke up, I felt almost no pain! I assumed this was because of the medications administered during surgery, but I was happy anyway.

We had arranged for an apartment where we would stay after the surgery, and when we got there, I went straight to the bedroom, lay down, and slept. When I woke up, I decided to get out of bed. I put my feet on the carpet and stood up—straight and pain free! I started walking, and I felt as though I was walking in the clouds. It felt like I was in heaven, and I was extremely happy!

In that moment, I remembered the promise of the scripture: "I will also ease the burdens . . . that even you cannot feel them upon your *backs* . . . and this will I do that ye may *stand*."

Upon my return home, friends came to greet me at the airport. I felt so loved. I knew many people in my ward had been praying for me, along with my family members. As the "broken piece," I had been surrounded by many wonderful and caring people who wanted only to help. These people were all witnesses to the tender mercies of the Lord that came into my life. I was filled with love and joy.

Another understanding settled over me. Perhaps the Lord wanted me to be the "broken piece" to teach me how to trust in Him too, to find physical healing as I explored the spiritual journey required by faith.

I know the Lord watches over us. He knows our sorrows, both physical and emotional. He knows how we feel. I am grateful for the painful experience I had. Although I realize there are others who suffer so much more than I did, I am grateful to have received my own special witness of the love God has for me. Now I stand with stronger faith and a deeper testimony. The Lord is our God, and He does visit us in our afflictions.

And sometimes He might require us to be the broken piece so we can become one with Him in purpose as He accomplishes His work in the lives of many people.

Ingrid Sanabria moved from Bolivia to Utah to attend Brigham Young University, where she graduated with a BS in integrative biology, and today she works as a global testing manager in a laboratory in Salt Lake City. She served a mission to the New York-New York South Mission. Ingrid met her husband, Rodrigo, who is also from Bolivia, while living in Salt Lake City. They have recently adopted two wonderful children: Luis, six, and Kaylee, four. In her spare time, she loves gardening, hiking, walking, swimming, writing poems, and spending time with family.

And now, O all ye that have imagined up unto yourselves a god who can do no miracles, I would ask of you, have all these things passed, of which I have spoken? Has the end come yet? Behold I say unto you, Nay; and God has not ceased to be a God of miracles.

—Mormon 9:15

$\mathcal{T}$WICE THE PERIL, TWICE THE MIRACLE
By Gina Shelley

When my dad received a job offer in a new state, it seemed like a fun adventure to graduate from high school early and journey with him to this new place for a few months before I began college. My mother and siblings remained behind to pack our belongings and sell the old house. Honestly, I was ready for a change. I had spent my whole life in the same town, with the same people, enduring the same drama. I jumped at the chance to do something new and exciting.

I soon found a job working in the local mall. One night, I closed the shop and faced driving home in the rain, which had been pouring down for the last hour. At 9:30 at night, in the blackness of evening and during a storm, I was very nervous about driving home. It wasn't that I was afraid of the rain, but being seventeen years old in the days before cell phones—and driving a yellow pickup that was also seventeen years old—scared me.

The truck was an old junker my dad had restored for his teenage kids to drive. It was already fairly beat up, an eye-sore, cheap, and something my parents wouldn't care about if it got a few extra dents in it as their teenagers learned to drive. Lucky me! I probably wouldn't have minded the yellow pickup so much if it had actually worked properly, but on that night, it was suffering from a few more mechanical issues than usual. Aside from the hole in the floor, where water would splash up on my feet when I drove over a puddle, the engine sputtered and sometimes died out completely if it got too wet. On top of that, the windshield wipers didn't work. Anticipating the drive home, I had good reason to be nervous.

I got in my car and said a prayer to Heavenly Father to help me get home safely. Because the rain was falling so heavily, I could barely see out the front windshield. I couldn't see the lane markers on the road or, really, anything else. I thought, *If I just follow the brake lights on the car ahead of me, I will know where to drive. I need to pay attention to the cars ahead of me.* With this strategy in mind, I started the pickup and began the perilous five-mile journey home.

I drove slowly and strained to see ahead. For the first few miles, I was doing all right and thought I might be able to make it home . . . until I remembered the bridge. The four-lane road narrowed to just two lanes on the old bridge, and it didn't have any lights on it. I knew I would need to follow another car if I was going to pass over it safely. Yet, the closer I got to it, the less traffic was on the road, and I found myself driving blind. I could not see the bridge ahead at all. The rain was still coming down hard, and my engine was sputtering. Just as the bridge materialized out of the dark, my engine coughed, sputtered, and died! I had no choice but to pull over to the side of the road and hope for the miracle of it starting again. I began to pray. *Heavenly Father, please help me get home safely. Please send someone to help . . .*

Soon after I ended my prayer, I saw three men emerge from a warehouse near the road. I kept trying to start the pickup, but it was useless. The three men quickly arrived at my truck, and one of them knocked on my window. "Hello? Are you all right?" The sight of them scared me, but I decided they were probably the answer to my prayer, so I rolled down my window. That was my first mistake.

"Hi. Um . . . my engine won't start. It quits on me when it gets too wet. Dumb, I know. It's a piece of junk, but if you could help, I'd really appreciate it."

"Go ahead and open the hood," one of the men said. "Let me see if I can do something to help." I reached under my steering wheel and pulled the lever that unlatched the hood. One of the men popped open the hood and looked at the engine. Meanwhile, one of the other men next to my door grabbed the handle, opened it, and began to lean inside. I assumed he wanted to try to start the engine. When he grabbed me, horror engulfed me. I began to fight back and started screaming for the other men to make him stop!

"Please! *Get off of me!* Leave me alone!"

"You know you like it, pretty girl. How are you going to pay us for helping to fix your car? We can have a good time together. Come on!"

Instead of stopping, he tried to climb inside the cab of the truck. As I struggled and tried my hardest to push him away, I detected alcohol on his breath.

"Help! Make him stop!" I screamed once again. "Leave me alone! Don't touch me!" With all the strength I had, I continued to push his hands and mouth away. The other two just stood by and watched. Finally, one of them said, "Come on, dude. Leave the girl alone. She doesn't want it."

"Shut up! She does too. Come on. Go around to the other side and help me hold her down!"

As soon as I heard him say that, I freed a hand and reached for the keys and tried the ignition. *Vrrruuumm!* The old truck started! *Thank goodness!* With the hood still up, two of the men blocking my view of the road, and the one man halfway on top of me, I shoved the stick shift into first gear, popped the clutch, then slammed my foot on the gas and didn't care if there was on-coming traffic. The pickup's wheels spun, throwing up mud as I blindly took off. The man fell back out of my car, and I grabbed the door and pulled it shut. I bounced over a few bumps and up onto the highway, which caused the hood to swing down and close—a small miracle in itself.

Sobbing, I couldn't see anything. The rain was still pouring as I miraculously made my way home with little-to-no visibility. "How could that have been an answer to my prayers?" I yelled out loud. I had never, ever been so frightened for my life or safety before, and I was shaking from head to toe. It was ironic since I had been raised in a large metropolitan area where I had always needed to be watchful but now found myself in this small country town where I thought I'd surely be safe.

When I pulled up to the empty house we had recently rented in anticipation of the rest of the family's arrival, I was relieved, but I didn't know what to do. I was crying and scared, and I had no idea how to tell my father what I had just been through. I hopped out of the truck and ran inside.

"What took you so long to get home?" my dad asked.

I didn't answer him but ran to my room, which had only a foam pad on the floor and a few blankets on it. I slammed the bedroom door and curled up on the floor. Dad could tell that something was terribly wrong. He picked up the phone and dialed my mother two states away to get some advice about how to talk to his crying teenage daughter. After several knocks on the door, Dad said Mom was on the phone and would like to talk to me. I felt ashamed and embarrassed. I felt stupid that I had been so vulnerable. However, as soon as I heard my mother's voice, I started sobbing all over again. Through choking tears, I managed to explain to her what I had just gone through. She told me I needed a blessing and that we were to call the bishop. "Mom, we just moved in here a couple of days ago! We haven't even gone to church yet! I don't even know him!"

"I don't care. You put your dad on the phone. We are going to find the bishop."

I handed the phone back to my dad, and they spoke a few minutes longer. I had to get out of the room. I felt dirty, violated, and abused. I went to take a shower to try to wash off some of the filth I was feeling, and I scrubbed and scrubbed as tears streamed from my eyes.

Soon the bishop and his counselor were at our door. Dad answered and, relieved to see them, invited them in. The bishop explained that my mother had called him long distance, and though it was nearly midnight, they had come to see if they could help a girl they had never met. Then he asked me how I was. I tried to tell them what happened. They stopped me after a minute. Since they had talked with my mother, they already knew. I was grateful I didn't need to say anything more.

The bishop, along with my father and his counselor, laid his hands on my head and began to administer a blessing of comfort to me. What I experienced next is hard to describe. Beginning at the top of my head, a beautiful feeling of peace and holiness began to sweep over my body. By the end of the blessing, my entire body felt renewed, cleansed, and healed. The evil and filthiness I had experienced was gone. The images that had been replaying in my head stopped. My horror was replaced with deep and healing peace.

This peace, which comes only from a loving Heavenly Father, stayed with me. I marveled long afterward at the completeness of the healing that occurred on that night. I felt great love for the men who responded to the call of a frantic mother two states away to please help her daughter. To have righteous men use the power of priesthood to dispel the evil intents of other men became a great and lasting testimony to me, not only of the existence of good and evil but also of the power of good to overcome evil.

We thanked the bishop and his counselors, and they quietly left, assuring me they would check back to see how I was doing. Then I hugged my father and told him I would be all right now. I knew the power of God had blessed me that night. And I knew there must have been angels watching over me—twice that night: first, the miracle of an old, stalled truck engine starting up when it did and, second, the priesthood blessing that healed my spirit. I could have felt betrayed and angry with Heavenly Father for not answering my prayers the way I thought He should have, but I never did. Evil and danger are all around us, but I learned that night that angels and the power of heaven are all around us too. What could have been a tragedy in my life became a witness that the Lord can help us find a way out of frightening situations.

Gina Shelley grew up in Las Vegas, Nevada, then attended Brigham Young University in Provo, Utah. She served a mission to Tegucigalpa, Honduras. Upon returning from her mission, she graduated with a bachelor of arts in education and began teaching high school English. She went on to earn a master of arts in English as a second language and a PhD in educational technology from the University of Utah. Gina and her husband, Brian, have four children. She loves to travel, read, camp, cook, craft, and sew.

Then hear thou from the heavens their prayer and their supplication, and maintain their cause.

—*2 Chronicles 6:35*

RANGER RESCUE
By Stephanie Daich

The first thing Mother heard after our car rocketed to a screeching halt, avoiding near disaster on the steep canyon road, was a bird. In the sudden quiet, its beautiful tune penetrated her soul deeper than a bird's song had ever done before. Her heart leapt with joy because she was alive! Her family was alive! Quickly, she herded us children out of the car and over the nearby embankment, where we would be safe. She gazed up at the sky to find the bird and noticed the trees rustling in the wind. As she reveled in the sounds of life, a breeze rushed through her hair, tickling her skin. The sensation was wonderful! There were so many colors blended together in the canopy. *Life* surrounded her.

I hadn't realized just how close to death we had been. I was young, only five years old that day. Excitement had filled the car that morning as my family had piled in, ready for our camping trip. We had been planning this trip for a very long time. For a whole week, our family would escape the fast pace of life and strengthen family bonds without worldly distractions.

After my dad did his final vehicle check, he kicked the tires and grinned in satisfaction. He had done his part in making sure everything was serviced, tuned, lubricated, inflated, and prepared for our long road trip. He checked the connections to the camp trailer and, behind that, our boat. Everything seemed ready. Dad climbed into the driver's seat and announced we were ready to hit the road. As soon as he shifted into gear, Mom yelled, "Stop!"

Dad hit the brakes. "What now?"

"We forgot to pray."

As we bowed our heads, reverence settled upon us. We prayed for the Lord to keep our home protected while we were gone, to help us kids get along, and, of utmost importance, to keep us safe during our trip. We placed great faith in our Heavenly Father, who understood our needs and desires, and knew He would keep us safe if it was His will. After the humble prayer, we were on our way.

What a sight we made! Dad's '74 Dodge Dart led our procession. In my five-year-old eyes, our car was hideous, with its mustard-yellow paint job. If our neighbors' attention hadn't been captured by the homely car, it would surely be captured by our ridiculous convoy, which included our thirteen-foot, two-wheeled camping trailer with its two-tone, yellow-and-green paint job, and the sixteen-foot Valco fishing boat rolling behind it. Perhaps towing two trailers behind us wasn't the smartest idea, but we were technically within the law. Besides, Dad had confidence that his Dodge Dart, with its V6 engine, could handle the job—which it more or less did at a snail's pace.

An uneventful drive led us to the ascent of a steep mountain pass that led from Vernal to Flaming Gorge, Utah. If the Dodge had proven slow on the freeway and highway, it was nothing compared to the sluggish climb we made up the mountain in second gear. But we finally made it to the top. Pride swelled in Dad's chest that his little car had met the challenge and succeeded. Thinking the most difficult part of our trip was now behind us, we began the descent.

When I first became aware that the car was swerving back and forth across two lanes, I was playing happily with my doll in the backseat of the car. I giggled because I thought Dad was trying to scare us. Mother immediately silenced me. Suddenly, I picked up on the high tension coming from the front seat. Something was very wrong.

The trailer and boat dangerously fishtailed behind us, and the force from the two trailers made controlling the Dodge nearly impossible. The car seemed to have taken on a mind of its own, rocketing down the road, heading toward a two-hundred-foot precipice. Tense with worry, Dad cranked the wheel as hard as he could to keep us from going over the edge. Mom later told me that she prayed a simple three-word prayer over and over, "Please, Heavenly Father. Please, Heavenly Father."

Just when it looked like we were going to head off the cliff, the car responded and began heading the other way, but the trailer and boat took longer to respond, which caused the wheels of the boat to skim the edge of the cliff, just centimeters away from disaster. If the wheels had gone over the edge, gravity would have pulled the boat, trailer, and our car down with it, but we missed it, just barely.

A new danger threatened now: the Dodge was headed straight toward the ridged mountain on the opposite side of the road. Miraculously, during this time, there was no oncoming traffic. Our unwieldy caravan rolled dangerously close to the rocky bank, barreling down the wrong lane, and I looked out the window and thought that if I rolled my window down, the mountain would pour into the backseat—that was how close we were to it.

That pattern of fishtailing between the rocky edge of the mountain and the opposite precipice went on for several long minutes until, finally, Dad brought the convoy to a stop in the middle of the road. With white faces, we all just sat in silence for a minute. That was when Mother first noticed the welcome song of the bird. Still shaking, we sat stunned, realizing we had just escaped probable death.

Then Mom realized we had stopped on the blind side of a curve. A new fear overtook her. That's when she ushered us out of the car and off the narrow road, leaving us with strict instructions to stay put.

As she climbed back up the embankment, several cars slammed on their breaks and madly swerved to avoid plowing into the boat. She ran to the other side of the bend, and, like a sentinel, stood in the middle of the road and began waving her arms to warn drivers that they needed to slow down.

While Mom was risking her life directing traffic, my brother took my hand and led me to a line of trees safely away from the road. Without any other way to help our parents, we decided to drop to our knees and pray. My sister told us to pray for a ranger. I poured my heart out in deep prayer, begging that it be God's will to send us one, despite the fact that I had no idea what a ranger was.

Meanwhile, Dad was up top working on the stranded vehicles. He later told us that he felt he was being directed on what to do. First, he noticed that both of the tires had come off the trailer! He went looking for the tires and found them close to the point where we started to lose control. Both tires were sitting side by side in a bush, just like someone had placed them there. On the other side of the bush was the two-hundred-foot precipice.

On the rims of the tires were huge holes where bolts should have been. He looked down at the axle and saw the bolts still connected to it. Enlightenment flooded Dad's brain as he realized what had happened. Prior to the trip, he had taken everything to the shop to be serviced. The mechanic must have tightened the rims onto the trailer with unusual force. Because he had likely overtorqued the bolts on the tires, the extra pressure probably caused the holes to stretch on the rims. With the bolts slipping away from the rims, the tires of the trailer had come off, and that was when Dad had virtually lost control of the car.

He felt impressed to put the spare tire on the trailer. Even though he only had one spare, he got out his jack and lifted the trailer off the road to make the one-sided repair. Just as he was tightening the last bolt, a man walked up and offered help. He was a ranger.

The ranger assessed the situation, then told Dad how fortunate we had been. He walked back up the road to his green truck, which was parked on the other side of the bend, then placed some flares to warn oncoming drivers. This relieved Mother of sentinel duty. He reached into the back of his truck bed and pulled out his own spare tire, although there was little chance his spare would fit our trailer.

Dad mounted the ranger's tire on the axle and tightened it—a perfect fit! Tears filled Mom's eyes as she realized how blessed we were. What were the chances that we would find another tire for our trailer so quickly? It didn't make logical sense that a truck's spare tire would fit our trailer, but it did fit, and the trailer was again ready to be pulled.

Dad checked over everything one more time. That was when he noticed two deep grooves in the blacktop about two to three inches deep, where the trailer had dragged behind without its tires. At one point, the grooves stopped. Dad said it looked like someone had picked the trailer up and carried it for thirty feet and then set it back down where our car had finally come to a stop. The section of road where it looked like we had been carried paralleled the steepest part of the cliff. Dad said a silent prayer of thanksgiving.

As we drove down the mountain, the ranger trailed behind us. When we arrived at the valley floor, Dad stopped, and he and the ranger examined the tires, which had already lost pressure. Dad pulled a pump out of the back of the trailer and pumped the tires back up. The ranger advised him where he could get replacement tires and where to leave the spare. With the situation looking safe, the ranger bid us good luck and went on his way.

We made it safely to Dutch John Campground.

Later, after finding two tires in a junk yard that fit perfectly, Dad returned the ranger's spare tire at the agreed-upon forest ranger station. There, Dad asked about the ranger who had stopped to help us. No one knew who he was talking about. He described our rescuer, then described his truck, and still, no one could tell us who had helped us that day. Disappointed that he couldn't personally thank the ranger for helping us, Dad left the spare tire at the station, as arranged, just in case the ranger stopped by to pick it up.

I learned the power of prayer that day. When I prayed for a ranger, I never doubted that one would come. However it came about that the ranger happened upon us, we all felt that God's hand was in it.

Mom truly realized the value of life that day and that we are not invincible, that life can be taken away from us at any second. She left that experience with joy and gratitude for life and with an unshakable faith in prayer.

And to this day, she clearly remembers the call of the bird announcing to her that life would go forward after all.

Stephanie Daich has a great passion for life, learning, writing, serving, dancing, and any opportunity to be out in nature. She shares these desires with her wonderful husband and her four incredible children.

Wherefore, I say unto you, that ye ought to forgive one another; for he that forgiveth not his brother his trespasses standeth condemned before the Lord; for there remaineth in him the greater sin.

—D&C 64:9

SOMETIMES WE DON'T KNOW WHY

By Pat O. Conover

July 3, 1971, is etched in my memory. Although it happened more than forty years ago, I still cry when I talk about that day.

It was a beautiful summer morning. I was a young married woman with two children: a girl, Christi, age four; and a son, Craig, who had just turned eight in May and had been baptized into The Church of Jesus Christ of Latter-day Saints in June. Life was good.

Craig and several of his friends had spent the night sleeping in our backyard, and Craig had still not changed out of the clothes he had slept in—jeans and a long-sleeved cotton turtleneck shirt—because he and his friends had been busy constructing a clubhouse out of old boards in one corner of our fenced yard. They had eaten breakfast and were now running around the yard, playing.

I was in the house when I heard the children screaming. I looked out a back window and saw Craig running around, his body engulfed in flames.

We found out later what had happened: two neighborhood children who were older than Craig had brought a smoke bomb to our house that morning. One of them had tried to light it, and it hadn't worked. He'd gone home, poured gasoline on it, and come back.

The boys had then gone into the small clubhouse they had built, and the older boy had again tried to light the firework. This time the gas exploded, and Craig was in the path of the flames. His clothes caught fire in the enclosed space.

When I looked out the window, I didn't wonder where the fire had come from, but in my sheer panic, before I ran out to the yard, I did manage to have enough presence of mind to grab a blanket from a cupboard.

I threw Craig to the ground and wrapped him in the blanket to put the fire out. At that point, I was so panic stricken I couldn't even think. It was then that a long series of miracles and blessings began.

A neighbor man who worked swing shift was home that morning and had also heard the screams. He was right there at my side, asking me where the keys to my car were. Our city didn't have an ambulance at that time, so we had to get Craig to the hospital ourselves.

A woman who also lived next door heard the screams too. She was there as I put Craig into the car, and for some unknown reason, she had a pair of scissors in her pocket and immediately cut Craig's shirt off. We found out later that if she hadn't done this, the material would have stuck to his skin and caused more pain when it was removed.

As my neighbor drove Craig and me to Utah Valley Hospital in Provo, Utah, about ten miles away, Craig was losing body fluids out of his burned flesh at an alarming rate. It was as if a hose was pouring liquid over his head.

Craig was burned over 60 percent of his body—mostly second- and third-degree burns. He was burned all around his torso, from the waist up, down the inside of his arms and down one leg, and his hair, eyebrows, and eyelashes had been singed off.

When we arrived at the hospital, they gave him a sedative, wrapped him in bandages, and told us we could take him home. I assumed they believed Craig was going to die and they couldn't do anything more for him.

By then my husband had been notified and was at the hospital too. He immediately called his uncle Dr. Levi Reynolds, who was a well-respected pediatric surgeon in Salt Lake City, Utah, another fifty miles north. Dr. Levi told us to bring Craig to Primary Children's Hospital, and he would meet us there. We put Craig in the backseat of our vehicle and drove to Primary Children's Hospital instead of going home.

Dr. Levi met us in the emergency room. He couldn't find a pulse in our son, and when he tried to insert an IV in many places on the unburned parts of Craig's body, it wouldn't go in. He was finally able to pump the IV fluid into a vein in one of Craig's ankles.

Craig later told us how, from outside his body, he watched Dr. Levi and the hospital staff working on him, trying to bring him back to life. He still remembers this experience vividly.

After four days in intensive care and many prayers said in his behalf—not yet knowing whether he was going to live or die—Craig was placed in a circular, rotating bed, where he spent the next two weeks. His arms were extended and tied to the bed so the nurses could turn him and relieve the pressure on his burns.

Because of the intense pain caused by trying to remove the bandages, Dr. Levi was not able to assess the burn damage for two long weeks. In all, Craig spent forty-five days at Primary Children's Hospital. During that time, he underwent surgery ten times to have the bandages changed and later to do skin grafting.

Dr. Levi had worked with burn victims during World War II and had even pioneered the burn treatments of that time. He knew how critical infection was with extensive burns. When it came to doing the skin grafts, he was right there, guiding the plastic surgeon.

They took all of the skin for the graphs off the upper portion of Craig's good leg and stretched it and patched it all around his torso. It was a very painful process. After many days, the doctors removed the dressings. If the graphs had taken, Craig would recover. To our joy, Craig's body had accepted all the transplanted skin! He was going to make it! Considering the extent of his injuries, this was a miracle.

During Craig's hospitalization, he received several blessings—from his father, grandfather, and other family members. He also received a blessing from Elder Henry D. Taylor, who was an Assistant to the Council of the Twelve at the time. Elder Taylor sensed something special in Craig and wrote us a note: "It is our hope and prayer that the Lord will heal him so he can lead those activities of normal life. I feel that he is a very choice little spirit."

One volunteer, Janis Noyce, cared deeply about Craig. She spent hours with him, especially when I couldn't be there. She fed him, read to him, played games with him, and took him for walks in the wheelchair. She brought him presents and genuinely loved him.

When Craig finally came home from the hospital, he was healed. He had extensive scars around his torso, on the lower side of his arms, on one leg, and under his chin, but miraculously, most of them were hidden under clothing. To this day, most people don't notice them.

The real miracle was how Craig dealt with his burns. He never let the experience prevent him from doing anything he wanted to do, and he never shied away from different activities. He played tennis in high school, became editor of his high school yearbook, worked on the stage crew throughout his junior high and high school years, and created his own disc jockey business at the age of fourteen, which he still runs on the side, employing many people.

The pain he endured and the hours of service given to him by the staff and volunteers at Primary Children's Hospital made him a better, more caring person. And he also touched their lives. For many years after Craig's accident, Janis sent him letters and cards for his birthday and holidays, always encouraging him. When she got married six years later, she invited Craig to come.

In some ways, this difficult challenge helped Craig prepare for a life of service. Not only did he serve a mission, but he has also given countless hours of service to his community in Springville, Utah, and is now serving a second term on the city council. He also serves his wonderful wife and their three children, two of whom have now married.

Why did this happen to Craig? I don't know. But I do know it changed our lives and especially Craig's. We could have harbored ill feelings toward the young boy who lit the firework. He was fourteen years old at the time and should have known better. But in the end, the important thing was that Craig's burns healed, and we were very blessed!

A few years ago, Craig had a second brush with death. He was diagnosed with non-Hodgkin's lymphoma. Doctors found a seven-pound tumor in his chest and gave him little time to live. He not only survived, but he also found that the chemotherapy and radiation had shrunk the tumor. He never even missed a day of work.

We can only wonder why Craig's life was preserved a second time. But for whatever reason, we are grateful to Heavenly Father for guiding all that happened—twice—to save his life.

Pat O. Conover graduated from Brigham Young University in clothing and textiles, married Martin Conover, and, with their son, two daughters, and two foster daughters, worked in the family newspaper business in Springville, Utah, for many years. She has been active in her community, serving on the boards of the Springville Museum of Art and the Springville World Folkfest. She is also a freelance commercial artist.

There is a space between the time of death and the resurrection. And now, concerning this space of time, what becometh of the souls of men is the thing which I have inquired diligently of the Lord to know.

—*Alma 40:9*

A GIFT FROM GRANDPA
By Lynne Anderson

As I entered the hospital room, I felt the general sadness and anxiety that flowed from family members circled around the hospital bed of a frail, beloved grandfather. He had been diagnosed with old-age leukemia months earlier and had now entered the final stages of his disease. There was nothing more anyone could do to halt the disease and no way, really, to comfort him. We held his hand and told him how much we loved him.

He gasped for every breath, and I will never forget how his rattled breathing stopped when he raised his head off the pillow, indicating he wanted us to stay. But visiting hours were over. Even though we knew the end was near, no one could know exactly when he would go. Grandmother wanted to stay with him throughout the night, but she was afraid to be alone with him. She was also exhausted and needed to sleep, so we all walked out of the room together. We didn't know, but I think he knew we would not see each other again in this life.

At the time, I wished I could stay with him and my grandmother, but it was growing late, and we had a long-planned-for activity scheduled for the following day. Surely grandfather would live one more day, right? I had drawn a tag for a buck on the Kennecott Private Reserve—a big deal in the hunting world, a tag many men would have loved to have. Not only did I have a tag, but I had to use it on opening morning—the next day.

My husband, Gerald, and I prepared our gear, then climbed into bed, all the time wondering if my dear grandfather would survive the night. When the phone rang at 4:00 a.m., Mother was on the line.

Grandpa had passed away just a few minutes earlier. It hit me hard—like a ton of bricks. The grandfather I loved and adored had truly passed away. He was *gone*.

Amid the sadness, I also felt happy because his suffering had finally ended. I realized the skinny, frail, bent-over man was no longer held hostage in a sick body. His spirit would now be tall, energetic, and full of life. This thought comforted me.

However, now I faced the challenge of going hunting, which was frightening because I was mourning the loss of my very beloved grandfather. Why today, of all days? My emotions were in turmoil, and I was a wreck, to say the least.

Gerald and I packed up and loaded the horses into our trailer and headed across the valley to our destination on the Oquirrh Mountain range. Perhaps we could find a buck quickly and get home so I could be with my family. The mountain ahead seemed tall, and I felt like with my luck we wouldn't find a buck until we got to the very top.

The mountain didn't have any trails, so we had to blaze our own. This meant we sometimes jumped over logs, crossed streams, plowed through bushes, and scrambled over rocks. My horse, Tango, was a cross between a quarter horse and an Arabian, which meant she had strong muscles and Arab quickness, but I was still reluctant because only the brave-hearted should ever attempt that kind of adventure. I did it because my husband, who loved hunting, was so thrilled that I had drawn a tag.

We slowly made our way up the mountain, climbing ever upward by a series of switchbacks. Gerald searched constantly for that prized buck, but my heart wasn't in it. I had only one thing on my mind. Where was my grandfather now? Had he left this earth and gone to heaven? Do spirits linger for a time? I began reminiscing about his life. My grandfather had been an avid hunter and fisherman. Every Saturday morning, he was up Provo Canyon fly fishing in the Provo River, wearing hip waders up to his elbows.

He also loved to hunt deer every year, and he took me with him on many occasions. As I rode up the mountain that day, I wondered if he knew where I was and that I was thinking of him. Could he be nearby, observing the trail, looking for deer? Was he proud of me for being a good sport on this day when my heart felt so heavy?

We reached the top of the mountain without spotting any deer and turned to go down the other side. While I mainly watched the footing of my horse on the steep slope, my husband watched for anything moving in the trees. Suddenly, he spotted a large buck! He pulled up and waited for me to catch up. We dismounted so as not to startle the buck, and Gerald tied up the horses and handed me the gun.

"Wait here," he said. "I'll go ahead and try to flush him out of the brush."

My job was to keep my eye pinned to the scope and get a good shot. It petrified me to be left alone, but I agreed. Gerald started walking forward, and I put the gun up to my shoulder and looked through the scope, trying to focus on anything that moved. I had my finger on the trigger, ready. Suddenly, to my amazement, the gun went off unexpectedly. I had not intentionally pulled the trigger.

Gerald came running back. "What did you shoot?"

"I didn't. The gun just suddenly went off." Shock coursed through me. Because I hadn't pulled the trigger with a clear shot ahead, who knows where an uncontrolled bullet might have gone? I could have shot my husband, who was out in front of me! I started to shake.

"Well, he's long gone now," Gerald said.

He and I climbed back onto our horses and continued on, looking for the buck. Deer usually hid, so maybe he wasn't too far away. We watched closely for any openings in the bushes ahead, waiting for him to reappear. Carefully, we headed down, going over fallen logs and under broken tree limbs and through small streams of water.

The beauty of the mountain seeped into my heart. Grandpa would love it here. Looking at all the fallen leaves, broken branches, and scattered rocks and bushes, I concluded that Mother Nature wasn't a very good housekeeper! But this environment was perfect for all of nature's animals to live together in perfect balance.

Many thoughts about Grandfather continued to fill my head. He had once been a pastor of a church and had been loved and respected by his congregation. I recalled how he often stood at the pulpit and preached a good, well-received sermon. And most of all, I remembered how much he loved his grandchildren. I was the oldest, and I kind of felt I might have been extra special in his eyes. I always felt his love and kindness. I would miss him deeply.

While my mind struggled with precious memories and pleasant thoughts of my grandfather, Gerald diligently searched for the buck. Suddenly, he spotted him sneaking along the ridge on the next draw over. The buck was close enough that Gerald thought I could get a good shot off. We dismounted, tied up the horses, and found an opening in the trees. I pulled up the gun and focused through the scope just as the buck appeared. I fixed on the target as I had learned to do and took the shot. He went down. I got my buck! It felt like I'd won a great victory.

Now we needed to make the long journey down the draw to get to the other ridge. I wondered how big he was and if I had a good one or not. As we got closer, Gerald dismounted and began searching through the brush. I held the horses. When we found him, we discovered he was big, one of most gorgeous four-point bucks I had ever seen.

Gerald turned him over. "He has two shots in him!" he exclaimed.

We later confirmed that both bullets had come from my gun! How could that be? Surely that first wild shot could not have hit the deer . . . could it? Puzzling over it, I became aware of the *presence of my grandfather.* A moment of sweet love filled me. Then another thought came. Had he in some way been responsible for that first seemingly wild shot that had found its mark?

I may never really know, but I have two bullets I treasure to this day that remind me of that very special moment on the mountain when I felt the comfort of having my grandfather's deeply loving presence close by—a final gift I will always treasure from him to me.

Later, at his funeral, I was his only grandchild willing to speak. I gave an in-depth life sketch, extolling his virtues and celebrating his love of life. Because of gospel teachings, I know one day I will see my grandfather again. Meanwhile, I am grateful for that moment on the mountain when I felt my grandfather's love. My heart had been grieving, and he comforted me.

Lynne Anderson lives happily in Sandy, Utah, with her amazing husband. She considers herself an organized perfectionist, a nail artist, a great cook, a good golfer, and an eternal optimist. She cherishes her health, her testimony, and her beautiful home. She loves people and has been blessed with the talent to create laughter.

My grace is sufficient for thee: for my strength is made perfect in weakness. Most gladly therefore will I rather glory in my infirmities, that the power of Christ may rest upon me.

—2 Corinthians 12:9

ℳY PAIN DRAINED AWAY

Name Withheld

From my toddlerhood up, I practically worshiped my dad. He was the smartest, wisest, most generous, most loving, and most forgiving person I knew—even when I became an exasperating teenager! As I journeyed through those years toward young womanhood, he stood by me, helping me, understanding me, and loving me all the way, as he also did with my several siblings. Through both his teachings and his examples, he showed us all what a true Christian was and how one should live. But I felt that he and I were especially close. He was my truest friend.

We could talk about anything, even delve deeply into spiritual, philosophical, and psychological topics. He allowed me to battle him intellectually about anything and showed an amazing patience and open-mindedness. He even admitted when I had a point he had not realized before. Many of our arguments/discussions took hours, but he never lost his temper at my rebuttals and never turned me off by pulling rank, and eventually, we always came to at least understand each other's points of view and sometimes even agree.

However, after I had been married a long time and lived far away, something strange happened to change our relationship. After my dad turned sixty, he began to grow suspicious of my words and deeds, becoming distrustful and accusatory. He no longer enjoyed my letters but wrote back attacking me for saying such "cruel and sarcastic things." It seemed that he twisted every word I said to bring out their worst possible inferences. So great became his distrust and fear of everyone that he would not even speak to some of my siblings.

I understand now that he may have had one or more silent strokes, tiny clots, or blood shortages that caused localized brain damage but showed no physical symptoms. They could have also caused personality changes and memory loss, but at the time, I had no idea about such things.

One day Dad wrote to me, asking in bewilderment why all the children he had loved and raised now seemed "out to get him." He asked me to please give him my views, since he could not understand what was going on and he knew I had delved deeply into psychology in my studies.

Now, *that* sounded like my *old* dad, seeking knowledge, being open to exploration, beginning a rational discussion. I wrote back that if my siblings were anything like me, they had become frightened of his change from a totally benevolent and open-minded father to a frequent writer of angry letters. I suggested that his behavior could possibly seem paranoid and urged him to see a psychologist for evaluation and treatment if necessary.

Within days I received a letter in return that scorched my very soul. He accused me of calling him crazy when it was obvious that I was not only the crazy one, but that I had also always been crazy and wicked as well! He remembered our closeness in the past as my desire to sexually seduce him. He said I was trying to destroy his marriage and the children still at home, then he lambasted me for every fault from A to Z and told me to never write or speak to him again, as he would burn my letters unread.

I cried for days at the unjust and baffling attack from my erstwhile best friend. He could not have wounded me more fiercely with a jagged butcher knife. My stomach churned, and I could not sleep for many nights. None of his accusations were even remotely true. I counseled with my husband, my bishop, and a couple of my siblings, who had also been cast from his favor. I spent hours in tearful prayer. But nothing eased my torn-up heart.

One afternoon, after aching from incessant weeping, I prayed aloud, "Heavenly Father, I cannot handle this pain anymore! You know I'm innocent of my dad's accusations. I've done everything I can to calm my feelings of hurt and betrayal, but nothing works. You know I'm willing to forgive, but the pain still won't leave me. Please, please, Father! With all my heart, I beg you to take away this pain!"

At that moment, it was as if a plug at the bottom of my soul got pulled. Starting from the top of my head, and progressing quickly to my feet, the pain drained down and away until I was empty of it! It had nothing to do with my willpower or effort and everything to do with the fact that the Lord had accepted my confession and plea: that by myself I could do nothing more and that I needed His miracle of atoning healing.

Oh, the relief! Oh, the joy that returned to my life! There were still family problems to work through until long after my dad's death, but I was able to forgive, understand, and truly let go of his accusations and my resultant pain. It never came back. I never again had to battle that issue.

Incidentally, I have begged the Lord at other times to remove this pain or that, but as long as there was work *I* needed to do and lessons *I* had to learn, the pain was not so easily taken away. I know the relief and joy that come from our Savior, who knows when to reach down into our lives and lift us when we can do no more on our own.

And whithersoever he entered, into villages, or cities, or country, they laid the sick in the streets, and besought him that they might touch if it were but the border of his garment: and as many as touched him were made whole.

—Mark 6:56

You WILL BE MADE WHOLE

By Dave Nichols

My wife, Deanna, and I own a cabin in Summit County in Utah. It was October 28, 2013, just before Halloween, and we were spending a few days there. I am the only living active member of The Church of Jesus Christ of Latter-day Saints in my family. My parents both died of cancer, my brother died when he was twenty-three, and just five months earlier, my dear sister, Kathy, who was my last living family member, had also passed away of cancer. I felt very alone, very vulnerable to the possibility of cancer, and very concerned about doing our family history now that the sole responsibility fell on me.

Spending time working at our cabin brought me much peace and comfort from the pain of missing not only my sister but also the rest of my family. I knew I would see them again, but I still missed them dearly.

That Saturday at the cabin, I was sweeping out the bed of the truck. The shell cover over the bed required me to lean over as I swept, and while I was doing so, the broom handle flipped back—hard—and struck me on my right cheek bone, causing a small cut that started to bleed. The blow dazed me, and I didn't feel quite right, but I cleaned my cut and continued to work.

The next day at church, I still felt odd, but I assumed things would improve in the coming days. On Monday as I talked with a close friend and work associate, he informed me that I was repeating things I'd already said, but I shrugged off his comments, making light of my broom accident and thinking the issues would pass.

The following Wednesday at work, I was reading an e-mail that I could not fully understand, so I called my work associate and asked for her feedback regarding what I thought was a poorly written e-mail. After reading the e-mail, she informed me that it was perfectly clear and well written.

The problem, then, was me. At her encouragement, I decided to drive to the emergency room to get checked out. Maybe I had given myself a concussion. I went in lighthearted. I joked about my ability to hit my head with a broom during the Halloween season, and the nurses laughed. I really thought it would be nothing.

As a precaution, they ordered a CAT scan on my head. After the CAT scan was completed, the emergency room staff turned somber.

"Is there something wrong?" I asked.

They told me the attending neurologist would come in to explain the findings. For the first time, I wondered if it might be serious.

My wife had arrived at the hospital in time for the doctor's initial assessment. He informed us that blood had hemorrhaged into the left side of my brain, and the resulting pressure had caused problems. The doctors wanted me to stay in the hospital for more evaluations.

Spending time in the hospital over a broom accident so close to Halloween continued to offer many lighthearted moments with the staff and many of my family and friends. After I spent several days under observation and in more tests, the doctors reached the conclusion that the blood would dissipate on its own and I would be back to normal in two or three weeks.

I returned to our home in Sandy, and days passed, but I did not feel I was improving. In fact, I tried to write out the alphabet but struggled to even do that. My reading ability was limited. I tried to be patient with the healing process, but by the end of the third week, I could see no improvement. In fact, things had gotten worse.

On a Saturday night while I was watching a college football game, I stood up and felt very dizzy and sick. I told my wife, "You need to take me to the hospital." Only I couldn't remember the word for *hospital* and told her to take me to *Hanukkah*. I knew exactly what I needed to say, but it didn't come out right.

We went to the emergency room—again. More tests followed, and again, they sent me home, this time around 4:00 a.m. on Sunday. I went to bed and continued to feel terrible. That afternoon the doctor called.

"I want you to go to the University of Utah Hospital. Now."

Deanna had been attending a rare work-related conference held on a Sunday, and all my neighbors were in church, of course, so I decided to drive myself. As I was driving out to the main road with my two daughters, Charlee and Delanee, I saw two ward members, Gerald Anderson and Dave Bytendorp, driving toward me. We all stopped.

Dave Bytendorp, my next-door neighbor, explained that he had been sitting in church when he felt impressed to leave immediately and give me a priesthood blessing. He had asked Gerald Anderson, another close friend, to help, and they had driven straight to my house.

I quickly explained the problem.

"We will drive you," Gerald said.

We all got into Gerald's car and headed to the hospital.

Once we got there and before any further evaluations were completed, Gerald and Dave finally had the opportunity to give me a blessing. It was beautiful and comforting. The doctors would be guided in my treatment. I was to pray to find out what I was to learn from this experience. And I was told that there was more for me to do upon the earth. I would be made whole, but it would take time.

That evening, with my wife and children in the room with me, the doctor told me what was wrong. Once some of the swelling had subsided in the brain, they had found a tumor. I needed to undergo delicate brain surgery.

This shocked all of us. The bishop soon arrived, as well as other friends. My daughter, Kylee, who was in college, drove all the way home to be with us. Unspoken fear bonded us all that night. Many in my family had now been claimed by cancer. Was it now my turn? Would I survive? Were these, in fact, the last days I would spend with my family?

That night after everyone left, I felt doubts, fears, and anxiety stalk me. I became aware of evil spirits telling me not to hope. I wondered if I had done enough in this life, and I felt I had lots of work I still wanted to do. I started to evaluate all aspects of my life. Perhaps I shouldn't have worked so many long hours. Perhaps I should have done this or that differently. I struggled with many fears. On and on it went, hour after hour. I remembered the verse from Alma, where he said, "I was racked with eternal torment, for my soul was harrowed up to the greatest degree"

(Alma 36:12). It was beyond horrible. I finally understood what it meant to be "buffeted" by the adversary.

I prayed all night long, pushing back against the darkness, grasping the promises made in the blessing I'd had earlier. I worried about my loved ones who had passed away. Who would do their work if I was taken now? What about my wife and children? What if I lived but became a burden to them all? The struggle against so much black hopelessness seemed endless. Toward morning, I finally slept.

I recall very little of the next two days. My condition worsened. I soon realized I could not read or write. What was I going to do? The words of the priesthood blessing came back once more. The Lord had work for me still. I would heal in time.

They scheduled my surgery for early Wednesday morning, the day before Thanksgiving. I found out later that the bishop asked ward members to fast for me. (See "Not Today of All Days!," 77)

The doctor came into my room Tuesday afternoon and was joking around with me. "Relax," he told me. "I've done this many times." He went on to say it had been a fortunate accident that I had been hit by the broom handle. Not only had it drawn attention to the growing tumor, but it may have also repositioned the tumor, making it easier to remove.

Tuesday night the bishop showed up, along with twenty of the young men from the ward. I had recently been released as Young Men president, and here they all were! We all knelt in prayer, even I did, and asked for the Lord's help to guide the hands of the surgeon in the morning. A strong power emanated from those faithful young men. When they left, peace settled over me. I was no longer nervous. Their visit, along with the prayers of many others, was very clearly making a difference in giving me and my family the comfort and faith we needed to carry on.

Early Wednesday morning I went into surgery. Hours later, I woke up. I had made it through and wanted to know where I was and what time it was. I couldn't stop talking, which turned out to be a good sign. The surgery had not affected my speech, anyway. The tumor turned out to be cancer—melanoma. The very word struck fear within me. I wanted to go online and read about it, but I had a strong impression *not* to do that. *Don't worry about it!* I listened to the Spirit and refused to do any research, and I once again held on to the promises I had received in the priesthood blessing.

Just a year and half earlier, a specialist had joined the Huntsman Cancer Center, adjacent to the university, and he was involved in pioneering new treatments for this kind of cancer. I would need only one radiation treatment and then several infusions of something called immunotherapy. It was not an easy process, but I felt sustained by the Lord and the love of many good people.

That sustaining power became evident during my only radiation treatment. I was alone in the room, strapped down, my head in a clamp, fighting claustrophobia, when I became aware of two personages dressed in white in the room with me. They seemed to be discussing what was happening, monitoring everything, making sure all went exactly as needed. Peace washed over me, and my fears left.

From that point on, I began a slow but steady process of healing.

One day in January, I attended the temple. It seemed a miracle just to be there. No one there knew I had had brain surgery. I was normal in appearance, and it felt wonderful. I thought about the journey I had been on for the last two months, and I was filled with overwhelming gratitude for the blessings of the Lord. I came to know how deeply involved He is in the details of our lives. I realized that many tender prayers had been answered. I knew He had blessed me with peace and comfort and healing.

Today I am back to normal. The experience taught me things I could not have learned without it, and for that, I will always be grateful. It has not been easy, but the Lord has helped strengthen my family and me throughout the process. I have been given a second chance, and I plan to use my time in the service of the Lord and my family in any way I can.

Dave Nichols and his wife, Deanna, live in Sandy, Utah. They are the parents of three girls, one in college, one in high school, and one in junior high school. Dave enjoys working with young men and Scouting and enjoys camping and spending time at his cabin.

We Feel His Love as We Keep His Commandments

"And we will prove them herewith, to see if they will do all things whatsoever the Lord their God shall command them."

—*Abraham 3:25*

THE SPIRIT OVERWHELMED MY REBELLION

By Lorie N. Davis

I am nothing if not outspoken, which at times can be a two-edged sword. I have a keen understanding of many things, so people rarely misunderstand what I say. Everyone knows I'm honest in my comments, and after they get to know me, they realize I'm also very loving; thankfully, because of that, they stoically endure and perhaps even occasionally appreciate my direct but sometimes tactless communications. It's not that I mean to be tactless; it's just that by the time I figure out how I should have said something, the opportunity to speak more gently has usually passed.

However, this trait evidently has its uses.

One day, the Relief Society president of my Detroit, Michigan, ward called upon me to help Janie (not her real name). Janie had been born a second twin and, deprived of oxygen at birth, acted a little backward in many ways. Now, at age forty, Janie still had the mind of a child and didn't seem to understand propriety in dress or behavior. Although quite overweight, when she was happy, she would skip down the halls at church, sing little tunes, and make inappropriate remarks in classes.

To add to all that, she had a seven-year-old daughter, Mindie, but did not have a clue about raising a child. The girl appeared to be quite neglected, not at all disciplined, and not even completely potty trained. Plus, she frequently got sick. Both mother and daughter often wore dirty, wrinkled clothing to church and smelled a bit ripe. It was no surprise that adults in the ward struggled to accept Janie, and the children in the ward avoided Mindie.

Upon visiting Janie's home, the Relief Society presidency found a disaster of dirt, spoiled food, piles of unwashed clothing and dishes, and spread-out accumulations of newspapers, school papers, books, and assorted trash. They may have tried cleaning her apartment before, but obviously what was needed was intensive *training* for Janie to learn how to keep house and raise her daughter.

Janie was way beyond tactful suggestions. What she needed was a kind but forceful taskmaster: *me*. The president decided I was the one to teach her incisively and directly what was right and what was wrong, clean and dirty, good and bad, healthful and harmful.

I went to work at the most elementary level. Picking up a spoon from the living room floor, I said, "Janie, everything must have a home. Where should this spoon live?"

She thought a while and responded, grinning, "In the spoon drawer!"

"Right! Good thinking! What if it's dirty?"

She looked around. "Um, in the sink?"

"Very good! Will you go put it there now?"

Happily, she skipped to the kitchen and added the spoon to the dishes in the sink.

"Now, Janie, how about these newspapers? Where should they live?"

"In a stack?" she asked.

"Are you going to read them again?"

"I don't think so."

"Then where should they go?"

"The trash!" And she ran to put them in the overflowing wastebasket.

After two hours of this, we had cleaned off much of the floor mess. "Janie," I concluded, "you have done wonderfully! See how much nicer your house looks? Do you think you can do this for an hour every day?"

"I know I can!" she replied enthusiastically.

I praised her for her great attitude and promised I would be back in two days to help her with the next step, which was learning how to do the laundry. But when I returned, Janie had done nothing more in the way of cleaning and had simply distributed more new junk over the previously tidy places. I started again to teach her.

Three times a week I went to her home to help and teach her. We bought detergent for dishes and clothes, and I taught her like a child to wash and rinse dishes and start the washing machine. I explained that she must never feed Mindie food that had been left out overnight because that was one way children could become ill. Unfortunately, I could see that in spite of her cheerful agreement, the minute I was gone, so were my lessons. She enjoyed my visits and attention, but no substantial change occurred. I became very discouraged.

After a month, the very thought of going to Janie's house brought on a throbbing headache. It was so futile! One night as I was praying, I assured the Lord that I was willing to do His will and follow His teachings, but I was worn out with trying to help Janie. Would He understand if I begged out of this obligation? I gave Him all the reasons it wasn't working and why it was becoming painfully difficult for me to keep it up.

Silence engulfed me. The hoped-for comfort didn't come. He didn't say yes. He didn't release me from this useless job. I could feel the silence in heaven.

I wept a few tears and pled for understanding. I even promised I would do *anything* else. The silence from above continued. Then into my mind came a quiet remembrance of my temple vows: to give my time, talents, and *all* the Lord had blessed me with to build up the kingdom of God. Finally, with drooping head, wet cheeks, and deepest sighs, I yielded my heart. I promised the Lord I would go back again and help Janie—and do so as long as He wanted me to, despite the uselessness of the task.

All of a sudden, the heavens opened and the full glory of the pure love of Christ descended upon me! I was filled with a soul-deep warmth and light that seemed to radiate from every pore of my body. I had never before felt that powerful love and adoring approval from my Lord and God. It reached every corner of my being, stretching my soul like an ever-expanding balloon full of radiant joy.

In that moment, there was no problem in my life that was of the least concern anymore. There was no harm that had ever been done to me that I didn't immediately and completely forgive as the most paltry nothing. There was no act or sacrifice on this earth that I would not do to please my Lord. There was no pain, no worry, just certain understanding of the overwhelming love of God. The feeling expanded, growing until I thought I would swell with love too huge for my body, for my room, for my house!

Soon I felt compelled to pray for the people in the ward, the people in my city, the people in the world, begging for mercy and love for them all. In that moment, I wished I could spread this gospel of joy to the whole earth. I felt as Enos described when his sins were forgiven. I understood Alma's gladness in his joys becoming as exquisite as his sins had formerly been painful.

Underneath it all, some part of me watched in awe, certain that if this went on much longer, I could not stay within the bounds of my earthly flesh; I feared I would be consumed. I prayed my praises, gratitude, and love for a long time until I faded into exhausted sleep.

I will never forget and never cease to praise the Lord for that transcendent experience! I *know* there is a God and *know* He loves me!

I did go back to help Janie for a few more weeks until they released the Relief Society presidency and then released me from that calling. Janie didn't change much then or later, as far as I knew. After a few months, she moved from the ward. But I learned how great in the sight of God people were when they were obedient and willing to give love and attention to "one of the least of these"—even though in my case, my head and heart had rebelled from doing it.

I recalled again the words from Abraham: "And we will prove them herewith, to see if they will *do all things* whatsoever the Lord their God shall command them" (Abraham 3:25, emphasis added). I learned that even small obedience is precious to the Lord, as bit by bit we pave our mortal way back into His presence.

Lorie N. Davis is a teacher, writer, storyteller, and instructional designer who has worked for BYU audio visual, LDS audio visual, and Southern Virginia University. She is a mother of three and grandmother of twelve. After her husband of twenty-two years passed away, Lorie served a proselytizing mission in Fiji. After returning home, she served an employment mission, specializing in résumés and scholarships. Lorie also admits to spending way too much time reading!

And, as it is written—Whatsoever ye shall ask in faith, being united in prayer according to my command, ye shall receive.

—D&C 29:6

$\mathscr{T}$HE TAXI RIDER

By Contessa Dotson

I drive a taxicab in Las Vegas—one of the few women who do. One day I was staging (waiting for a fare) at the south mall behind a long line of other taxis, and I was about to drive to another place to see if I could find a fare but felt compelled to stay at the mall. So I did. I eventually made it to the front of the line, and a nice-looking man in his thirties got in.

In a friendly way, I asked him how his day was going. I noticed he had a European accent and realized he was traveling abroad. I asked if he and his family were having a nice vacation in Las Vegas.

He explained that he was on a business trip and that this was his first time in the United States. As I drove him to his hotel, he said it had taken him many days to get his visa to come into the country, and now that he was finally here, he was amazed at how friendly and happy everyone was. "You are also very friendly and kind," he said. "What is this happiness I am seeing and noticing here in America?"

"I'm not sure what it is for other people, but for me, it's because I go to church," I responded.

He asked what church I attended.

"The Church of Jesus Christ of Latter-day Saints." He had a slightly puzzled look on his face, so I added, "We are also called the Mormons."

His face lit up in happiness. "I have heard of this church. Do you believe in Jesus Christ?"

"We do. We believe in God the Eternal Father, in His son Jesus Christ, and in the Holy Ghost."

He pulled out a picture of Jesus he had in his wallet. "See, I believe too."

"That's wonderful," I told him.

I always carry the Church's pass-along cards with me in my taxi, and I felt I ought to give him one. I actually gave him two. I told him the picture on one was the Salt Lake Temple.

"Beautiful," he said.

The other had a picture of Jesus Christ on it, which he lifted up and kissed.

Then he turned the cards over and read their backs. Among other questions on the cards were "What is the meaning of life?" and "Where do we come from?"

We talked, and this man was so excited that he could hardly sit in his seat. He was in the middle of the backseat and leaned as far forward as he could to take in all this wonderful new information. As I spoke to him about our beliefs, the Spirit was strong, and I could barely hold back my tears.

I was smiling and felt so happy the whole time I was talking to him. Seeing someone that excited about the gospel was a wonderful feeling. As we neared his hotel, he said, "I want to bring my family here and experience this happiness. First my wife, then my two children."

"That would be wonderful," I said.

It was a soft and sweet moment. I thanked him, and I wished so much that I had a Book of Mormon to give him. I explained that he and his family could look up LDS.org and invite the missionaries to his home.

He said he would do that, then added, "Now I know why I was meant to come on this business trip here to America. It's the happiness I have experienced. I have never felt this way before." He paused, then said, "I want you to know that I have won in Las Vegas."

"What do you mean?"

"I won in Las Vegas because I meet you," he said, slipping slightly in his English.

I was so touched I almost couldn't speak. "Thank you."

It was such a sweet thing to say to me that after he paid for the ride, closed the cab door, and waved good-bye with a most happy smile on his face, tears rolled down my cheeks. He was such a nice, pleasant person, and we had shared a sweet outpouring of the Spirit together. Just sharing a little about the gospel helped me realize what kindness, cheerfulness, and happiness the gospel can bring into someone's life.

My husband, John, and I are currently ward missionaries. We are thankful for this rewarding calling. We pray often to have missionary experiences. In D&C 29:6, we read: "Whatsoever ye shall ask in faith, being united in prayer according to my command, ye shall receive." I felt meeting this gentleman from Europe was an answer to prayer.

Seeing others happy and teaching the gospel is wonderful. I am glad I waited at the mall that day. The Lord really is watching over all of us, and on that day, a stranger to me—but not to God—visiting from a foreign country, found out where he might look for happiness.

Contessa Dotson lives in Las Vegas with her husband, John, who is her best friend. They enjoy dancing, swimming, roller blading, traveling, and just doing fun things together or with their large, extended family. Contessa is currently studying to get her culinary/pastry degree and loves to design fashion apparel and wear 1930s hats.

Choose you this day whom ye will serve.

—Joshua 24:15

A DECLARATION OF COURAGE

By Paul Fowles

As the stake Sunday School president, I often visited various wards, sometimes dropping by a classroom to observe the implementation of the curriculum. I have been impressed with the excellence of the teaching, and I've seen some encouraging results.

On one particular Sunday, I attended a class where four or five boys arrived late. One, who appeared to be the leader of the group, stood out for some reason. I motioned him to come sit beside me. The teacher showed a video entitled *Sanctify Yourself* by Elder Jeffrey R. Holland of the Quorum of the Twelve. Elder Holland's message impressed me. He spoke about times when we may find ourselves in frightening and even perilous moments, and our faith and our priesthood will demand the very best of us and the best we can call down from heaven. He said the day might come when a time of critical need would arise and we would need to be spiritually prepared.

I gave some thought to this concept. To be prepared to stand up and be counted on in times of critical need, we first need to be prepared and worthy to have courage to stand for who we are in ordinary circumstances. A story came to mind, and I felt I ought to share it with the latecomer. After class I asked to speak to the boy.

My son Jared and his wife, Candace, flew to Louisiana to settle her father's estate, I explained. Jared had to return early to his job in Utah, so he left Candace to tie up loose ends. As Jared waited for his flight, he recognized Elder Jeffrey R. Holland, who was also waiting to take the same flight to Salt Lake City.

Jared had never spoken directly with a General Authority and wasn't sure if it was even appropriate to do so. But inside he knew he could look this man in the eye and not fear what Elder Holland might see in him.

He mustered his courage and introduced himself. They exchanged a few pleasant words, and that was all. It was a small moment, perhaps, but as I told the story, I hoped the young man understood that choices he made now would determine his worthiness to step up in unexpected moments.

Afterward, I reflected on what it took to find the courage to do hard things. I realized I had learned to stand up for the Lord, not only in times of great need or peril but also in the seemingly ordinary events of life. One of the first memories I have of calling on courage happened in the winter of 1973. I was serving in the Kansas Missouri Mission and had just been transferred to Platteville, a small college town in rural Wisconsin. The Kent State shootings in Ohio had recently made headlines, and many college campuses were rife with discontent. When my companion and I were asked to proselytize on the university campus, I cringed. The thought of approaching the students terrified me.

The first Tuesday in my new area, we had to walk one mile to campus. With each step, my dread increased. My companion explained that we would talk to students as they walked to their classes. Of course, I assumed my companion would do the talking.

Then my companion gave me some copies of the Book of Mormon and said, "The students will talk to you." Then he turned away! It was clear what he expected me to do. With a prayer in my heart for courage, I approached a student. I explained something about the Book of Mormon, and he accepted one! There was no riot, no explosive words, and my fears suddenly vanished.

In that moment, I learned something about courage: if I would do my part, the Lord would help me. By the end of the day, my companion and I had set up several appointments, and one of them led to a baptism.

Another seemingly small challenge came during my early days of military service when I was called to attend a staff meeting. In attendance were several officers who outranked me by two or three ranks. As the meeting progressed, each staff officer took a turn to relate events under his command. My duty was to take notes and report back to my superior officer.

At that point, the officer in charge of personnel began talking about items of concern outside the base. Suddenly, out of the blue, he asked,

"What about the Mormons who live on base?" I froze. I was junior to all of these important men. What was the protocol in this situation? It was not expected for someone of my rank to speak at all. The easy and safe road was to say nothing. Yet . . . I had the information these men needed.

Gathering my courage, I spoke up. "Sir! I am a member of the LDS Church." I then related to these men the location of the meetinghouse and the name of the bishop. I stated I would be happy to answer any questions after the staff meeting. My answers must have been satisfying because there were no repercussions after the meeting.

Standing for who we are at all times and in all places can take courage.

I have learned that being worthy to speak up and actually doing it, even when I feel fear, brings blessings. I am grateful for the small lessons of life that have taught me to stand firm in the Lord's service. And I hope the young man who drifted into class late that day will begin to make those small decisions now that will help him develop the courage to stand for who he is later on when faced with challenges yet to come.

Paul Fowles was born in Delta, Utah, where he continues to live today. He served a mission to the Kansas Missouri Mission and then attended Utah State University. Upon graduation, he was commissioned a second lieutenant through the ROTC. After years of service, he retired a lieutenant colonel from the National Guard. He is married to the ~~late~~ *Anna Lenore Anderson of Spanish Fork, Utah. They have five children and seven grandchildren.*

And all thy children shall be taught of the Lord;
and great shall be the peace of thy children.

—*3 Nephi 22:13*

WALKING IN THE LIGHT OF SUNBEAM LOVE

By Maureen J. Knapp

I was called to teach the three-year-old Sunbeam class in Primary. It surprised me to learn that there were fourteen children in my class, which is a lot of children in one class! I was told not to worry because on any given Sunday only about three or four attended.

I accepted the calling and went home, thinking about how to begin. Ordinarily I would have made it a top priority to visit the children and their families to get to know them. However, there were so many that just the thought of visiting fourteen children in one week overwhelmed me. Besides, they were only three years old.

Three days went by, and I began to feel uneasy. I knew I was not doing the best I could in this new calling. Finally, I started the process of making visits and getting to know the children and their parents. So many children and so little time! However, meeting them proved to be very enjoyable, and I felt I had made new friends.

By Saturday, I still had three children on my list that I had not been able to meet. Because I had done my best, I thought it would be acceptable to the Lord. Eleven children visited in just three days! I'd worked hard to get so many, so why did I still feel uneasy? Again I tried to reach the other children. By 8:00 p.m., I had visited all but one little girl. I decided this would *have* to do. Then, as I was walking home, a car drove past me. I turned around to see where it was going, and it pulled up to the home of the very last child.

I turned around and walked quickly back the way I had come. As the mother unloaded groceries, I introduced myself as her child's Primary teacher. I explained that I was excited to have her in my class.

I found out the mother was not a member of the Church and the father was less active. She and her husband explained that they did other activities on Sunday, so their daughter would not be coming to Primary. Besides, the mother explained, she didn't even own a dress! No, they would not be coming.

I bent down close to the little girl and told her I would miss her and that Heavenly Father loved her. I thanked the mother and said she would be welcome anytime she might have an opportunity to attend.

On the way home, I felt good! Maybe even a little prideful. After all, I had done it! That night before I went to bed, I knelt and talked to Father in Heaven and told Him I had done all I could and if the children were to attend the next day, I needed His help to touch the hearts of the children and their parents.

Sunday morning came, and as I arrived at the Primary room, I saw one row of five chairs set up for the Sunbeam class—one for the teacher and four more for children. Why, that was ten chairs short! I quickly arranged two more rows of chairs. A member of the Primary presidency became aware of what I was doing and quickly counseled me not to feel too disappointed when the chairs went unused.

Then the miracle began. One by one the children came in looking scared. But when they saw me, they smiled and came forward. I hugged each and every one of them. First, four arrived and the front row of chairs filled. Then four more came. Then two more. Finally, thirteen children had arrived. Only one chair remained empty. The last child I'd visited had not come.

I felt happiness and sadness at the same time. The music began, and the Primary president stood to conduct. Then the door to the Primary room opened, and the last child stood hesitantly there, searching with frightened eyes for a familiar face. I stood and held out my hand. She came forward, and as she placed her hand in mine, I looked up at the Primary president and saw tears in her eyes. I looked back, and in the hallway stood the mother, wearing a dress! She did not come inside the room but remained in the hall, listening to the children's talks, the sharing time presentations, and the music.

After opening exercises, she followed us to our classroom. I invited her in, but again she refused. She waited by the door until class ended. This became a pattern. The mother brought her child, then waited in the hall. After months of this, one day she ventured inside the Primary room and stood at the back.

Most importantly, from that very first day, except for illness or vacations, all the Sunbeams attended regularly for the entire year.

During that year, the Primary song "Teach Me to Walk in the Light" stood out to me. These children were learning to walk in His light, learning to pray, and learning to do what was right.

Eventually the children turned four, and I asked if I could remain their teacher. The single row of chairs remained three rows of wiggly little children. Gradually, the mother of the little girl grew more confident, sometimes standing at the back of the room, sometimes dropping off her child, knowing her daughter was walking in the light of love.

About four years passed, and during that time, the young girl's parents were befriended by their LDS neighbors. One day the girl and her parents showed up for sacrament meeting with their neighbors. They began to attend the block, and when the little girl turned eight, they gave permission for her to be baptized. Two more years went by, and then the neighbor told me the mother was ready for baptism too!

I knew then that *everyone*, even a young child, is important to Heavenly Father. He loves all of us, and sometimes His plan to reach into our hearts can begin with something as simple as a Primary teacher who loves a little Sunbeam.

My memory went back to the week when I felt it was just too much to ask that I visit every single child in my class before Sunday. I had always been taught we were to *magnify* our callings—put in a little more effort than called for. So the persistent feeling of needing to see *all* of the children finally touched my heart sufficiently that I had no peace until I had seen them all. It came to me that Father in Heaven had trusted me with a very sacred calling: teaching the Sunbeams.

Maureen J. Knapp lives in Sandy, Utah, with her husband, Jerry. They have six children and seventeen grandchildren. Maureen enjoys teaching others about cooking with food storage ingredients, baking whole-grain and white breads, and mastering dutch oven cooking. She is a member of IDOS—International Dutch Oven Society—where she is often called on to judge dutch oven cook-offs.

Cast thy burden upon the Lord, and he shall sustain thee.

—Psalms 55:22

$\mathcal{N}$OT TODAY, OF ALL DAYS!

By Judy C. Olsen

The week of Thanksgiving is always busy. Even though my children are now grown and on their own, we still often gather at Thanksgiving. This particular year was my turn to host the family on Thanksgiving Day. One of our long-held traditions, begun when the children were very young, was serving pie for breakfast on Thanksgiving morning. Believe me, pie tastes wonderful when you are hungry.

Although I could have bought pies, I never did. As a new bride, I stumbled on the perfect pie crust recipe that made a light and flavorful crust that melted in your mouth. I felt so confident in my pie-making skills that I usually baked six to eight pies every year.

Wednesday was always my pie-making day. Even during my working years, I took off the Wednesday before Thanksgiving to bake pies. It was tradition.

This particular year, just before Thanksgiving, two things happened: First, my oldest grandchild, Rachel, who was sixteen, wanted to come to my house, spend the night, and learn how to bake wonderful pies. In fact, she wanted to know how to cook the entire dinner! She planned to be at the house by 10:00 a.m. on Wednesday and stay through Thanksgiving.

That same week we heard that our neighbor, Dave Nichols, had just been diagnosed with a brain tumor. (See "You Will Be Made Whole," 51) I recall thinking *How awful, especially during the holidays!* I hoped he would be okay.

On Tuesday I had a lot of shopping, planning, cleaning, and cooking to do. After running around most of the morning, I grabbed a light lunch consisting of nothing more than a small tossed salad, then I headed off to the grocery store. I spent a lot of time and money and finally thought I had everything ready for pie making on Wednesday and dinner on Thursday.

Taking a breather, I sat down at my computer and turned it on. I saw an e-mail from our Relief Society president, and I clicked on it, expecting an update on Dave Nichols, which it was. He was in the hospital, and he would be undergoing brain surgery in the morning. Then came the words, *The bishop has asked us to fast for him as a ward on Wednesday and again on Sunday* (which was fast Sunday).

I stared at the screen. Not tomorrow, of all days! I'd be in the kitchen for many hours. I had a granddaughter coming. He could have surgery any day of the year . . . but fast tomorrow? Really?

Many things went through my mind, including, *I have a lot of good reasons to refuse to fast; others will fast, and that will be sufficient.* But other thoughts also came to me: *What if I were the one sick on a holiday? Would I hope someone would fast and pray in the hour of my need?* Not to mention, it was the bishop asking. He wouldn't ask unless he felt it was seriously needed.

I felt an enormous burden fall on my shoulders. On top of everything else, this too? I wondered if it would even be possible. It was 3:30 in the afternoon. If I ate dinner and started my fast afterwards . . . no. I'd have to fast *all day* Wednesday while working with food. Plan two: what if I began *this very moment?* Then I could fast from lunch to lunch; that might work. But all I'd had to eat for the last many hours was a small tossed salad. I'd be starving in no time. Plus, I wouldn't be able to prepare my body for a time of fasting. No last drinks of water. No good meal.

I bowed my head, and as I explained to the Lord my problem, tears filled my eyes. All these people coming! A beloved granddaughter to teach! A great deal of food that needed preparing! And . . . a very sick friend and neighbor. I asked the Lord to bless and sustain me, and with tears now falling, I started my fast that very minute. It was the only way.

I then turned to all the things I needed to do. Somewhere around bedtime I stopped and realized I was neither hungry nor thirsty. And I had lots of energy. I went to bed and the next morning got busy preparing everything for the arrival of my granddaughter.

Somewhere around midmorning I realized I didn't feel weak, tired, hungry, or thirsty. Maybe last night's good feeling was believable, but now? Nearly twenty-four hours since my little salad? I couldn't recall a fast, ever, where I'd felt so full of energy as I neared the twenty-four-hour mark.

My granddaughter arrived, and we started mixing ingredients for the pie crust and frosting the edges of fluted dessert dishes with powdered sugar; then we moved to mixing pie fillings. As noon approached, I had her roll out a crust and explained that I was fasting and needed to go say a prayer.

I went to a quiet place in my home and asked Heavenly Father to bless Dave, that if it was His will, all would go well. Then I returned to the kitchen and had lunch. Rachel and I spent a long, exhausting day on our feet, but I never felt tired. My back, which often hurt when I was on my feet, didn't hurt. The usual post-fast letdown of energy never materialized.

The next day the two of us cooked, set a lovely table—including our frosted fluted crystal salad cups—and prepared all things for dinner. Guests arrived. I went from kitchen to table to individual people, helping, serving, coping, solving problems, seeing to everyone's needs. After dinner we talked, laughed, played games, and spent a wonderful day together.

Friday came. We heard that Dave had come through his surgery with flying colors, and I noticed something else: I was almost too weak to move!

Suddenly, I understood the lesson I had been given. At a time when fasting would have been very difficult, I had gone ahead and done it, only asking that the Lord sustain me throughout my time of fasting. But He had done more than that. He not only sustained me throughout my fast, but He also sustained me all day Wednesday and all day Thursday! I had received back double what I had given. But now that the need was gone, I had been left on my own to recover. Tiredness engulfed me, and I could hardly move for hours! The contrast was striking.

Fasting can be hard and is not my favorite thing to do, but on that day, I knew the Lord was deeply aware of my righteous desires and blessed me abundantly for my efforts. I am grateful to the Lord for sustaining and helping me during one of the hardest days of the year to start a fast. And I am grateful that my prayers, as well as those of other ward members, were heard that day on behalf of a friend.

Judy C. Olsen lives in Sandy, Utah, with her husband, Donald. They have four children and eighteen grandchildren. Judy enjoys writing, teaching in the Church, sewing, and drawing. If you would like her never-fail pie crust recipe, go to her website: olseneditorial.com.

God shall give unto you knowledge by his Holy Spirit, yea, by the unspeakable gift of the Holy Ghost, that has not been revealed since the world was until now.

—D&C 121:26

$\mathscr{A}$ PROMISE FULFILLED

By Lon Pearson

When I was twelve years old, I received my patriarchal blessing. One of the promises I was given at that time was the assurance that if I would prepare properly, I could achieve the fulfillment of many marvelous promises: "You will be blessed with the gifts of the Spirit . . . and you will have visions *so that you will understand men*" (emphasis added).

At age twenty I was called to serve in the Mexican Mission for two and a half years (1959 to 1961). With about six months remaining, I was assigned to serve in the port city of Veracruz, on the Gulf of Mexico, where the Church had been growing at the amazing rate of one hundred converts a year, leading the entire Church at that time.

On a Sunday evening late in January 1961, we learned that the married son of one of our members had gone to the Red Cross Hospital. We immediately headed there, where we found Sister Fernández at his bedside. Mario, who had begun taking the missionary discussions, had been shot in the stomach by a .22, and the bullet had not yet been removed. He was in bad shape.

Mario's mother requested that we give him a priesthood blessing. We anointed and blessed him and then continued to visit Mario throughout the week. His outcome did not look good.

The following Monday afternoon, we went to the hospital once more. About 5:20 in the afternoon, the nurse let us in to see him. The doctor who attended him asked us to wait. As we stood quietly, we watched as Mario took his last breath and passed from this life.

That was my first time witnessing death, and it was a traumatic experience for me. What made it worse was that just as Mario died, a

Catholic priest rushed in and chastised the hospital staff for not calling him sooner to administer the last rights of his church. His anger and attitude disturbed me, as it seemed out of place at that sacred moment when a soul had just crossed through the veil.

We walked out to the waiting room, and when we informed Mario's mother of his death, she became extremely distraught. My companion and I tried to help her, and we finally took her home in a cab and notified the branch president. Later on, our district president arrived and gave her a blessing, commanding her to sleep, which she finally did. The entire evening had been a shocking emotional experience for all of us.

The next morning, a Tuesday, we went to visit Sister Fernández. She continued with her agitated behavior but gradually calmed down. That afternoon we held Mario's funeral in the new district chapel. I knew the Atonement and our understanding of the hereafter gave us a different view of mortality and of passing on; yet I still felt deeply shaken.

I had witnessed death—the tragic outcome of a murderous act—and wondered in my mind why a young man, wanting to turn to God, seemed to have been abandoned by Him. I knew and loved the Fernández family, and I tried to resolve the questions of their eternal status in my mind. That night, I had a dream in which I witnessed Cain approaching Satan and making a covenant with the evil one. I stood close to them, and they talked vociferously at times. At other moments, though, they spoke in hushed tones, making signs as if entering into a wicked covenant. Our common enemy, the devil, exercised such great power over Cain that I felt terror in my soul. I backed away a bit, almost hoping to zoom out of the horrible scene I was witnessing, and when I became aware once more that I was in my own bed, I immediately rolled out and grabbed the arm of my companion, who was sleeping in the bed across from mine. I pleaded with him to get down on his knees and pray with me.

Somewhat confused, he knelt with me as I poured out my heart, aloud, asking that my companion and I might be protected from that moment on from any evil forces such as I had just witnessed. I fervently prayed that we might be preserved from the terrible power of Satan and his attacks.

That sincere prayer brought me solace. Perhaps just as important, I had seen in vision events that would help me understand men—as promised in my patriarchal blessing. It opened my spiritual eyes. I vowed that I would *never* let Satan take control of my soul.

I turned to my companion and expressed to him my appreciation for his joining me in prayer at that moment of Satanic terror. Today, there is no doubt in my mind that there are powers that can influence men—for good or for evil—according to their desires.

Lon Pearson is a retired professor of Spanish, having taught at UCLA, where he earned his doctorate; at the University of Missouri–Rolla; at the University of Nebraska at Kearney; and at Brigham Young University. University research projects have allowed him to visit most of Latin America. He has been called as a bishop twice for a total of nine years. He and his wife have served senior missions, including returning to Mexico to teach institute, and they have served in two temples since 2009.

Trust in the Lord with all thine heart; and lean not unto thine own understanding. In all thy ways acknowledge him, and he shall direct thy paths.

—Proverbs 3:5–6

WHAT CAN I DO?

By Frances Pershing

Shall I pay tithing or buy food and pay the bills?

It was hard after my divorce. I not only had to support myself, but I also had to support my daughter and her baby (she having divorced an abusive husband) as well as my son, who was trying to clean up some problems in his life so he could serve a mission. Although we were all employed, none of us had high-paying jobs.

I didn't know how to juggle everything. My daughter and son tried to help as much as possible, but the bills just kept coming. Even then, tithing was a necessary commitment in my life, and I paid it faithfully. No matter how little we had, I always paid tithing.

One day the electric bill came, and there was no money anywhere; we had hit a wall. It was hot most of the year in Arizona, and the demand for air conditioning got expensive. I put the bill aside, hoping I could get the funds to pay it plus other expenses we were incurring. Finally, one day I came home from work to a very hot, dark house and a notice on the door that said my power had been shut off due to nonpayment. It was several days before payday, and I had no money in the bank. None of us had any extra funds floating around. I worried most about the baby's welfare and losing what little food we kept in the freezer, as I had no money to replace it.

My only resource right then was to kneel at my bedside and tearfully ask for help. I poured out my heart to Heavenly Father. *What do I do?* Tears streamed down my face. I was crying so hard that I could hardly ask for help. I needed to pay the bill, but how? Then quietly, as though someone was in the room with me, a voice said, "Be of good cheer, my daughter."

Be of good cheer? The words resonated with my spirit, and I knew without a doubt that somehow the check I would write would be honored. I ended my prayer, got my purse, and went to the utility office, which was still open. I wrote a check for the full amount, including an additional fee for turning the power back on. I had no idea what would happen next, since there was nothing in the bank to cover the check, but I had been told to "be of good cheer."

The next day, in the mail, my income tax refund arrived, which I had not been expecting for another several weeks.

Tithing is still top priority in my life. It is my safety net. I know that when I do all I can to manage, the Lord will open doors to help.

Frances Pershing was born in Idaho, grew up in Wyoming (Green River and Rock Springs), and then attended BYU. She got married in Arizona and raised two children there. Frances had five grandchildren and four great-grandchildren. She lived in North Carolina, where she enjoyed spending time with family, writing stories and poems, and painting until she passed away in December 2014.

Whosoever therefore shall humble himself as this little child, the same is greatest in the kingdom of heaven. And whoso shall receive one such little child in my name receiveth me.

—Matthew 18:4–5

HE WANTS TO TAKE YOU ALONG

By Michael D. Young

I remember the first time I saw my son Bryson. The ultrasound showed nothing more of the little guy than a grainy, black-and-white image on a screen, but I knew right away that I was going to love him. What I did not know were the hardships he would have to face during his first year of life.

Though my wife, Jen, had several tests and ultrasounds throughout her pregnancy, we had no idea about Bryson's Down syndrome. He came into the world at 3:00 a.m. on November 1, very tiny . . . and not breathing. The nurses whisked him away, and one came to my side to speak to me. In hushed tones, she told me Bryson exhibited some of the physical markers for Down syndrome but that further testing would be needed to determine whether that was the case. We couldn't hold him because he was hooked up to so many machines and tubes, and before we knew it, an ambulance had whisked him off for what would be forty days in another hospital in Salt Lake City, an hour away from our home.

When we were finally able to see Bryson again late that night, he was covered with bandages that protected the gaping opening in his abdomen caused by a birth defect, and he had wires and tubes attached all over his tiny body. We still could not hold him, but the doctors agreed that we could touch him if we prepared properly. These preparations included a vigorous washing, scrubbing our hands and arms up to our elbows, and cleaning under our fingernails with plastic picks.

We knew his first days would include surgery to fix his abdomen, so I called my three brothers and asked them to help me give Bryson a priesthood blessing on that first night of his life. We each placed only a finger or two on his little head, and I gave him his first father's blessing.

To our frustration, the surgery kept being delayed, and we found that he was not strong enough to take food through his mouth. Instead, they fed him through a slender tube inserted through his nose. I visited him whenever I could, especially enjoying the one-on-one visits I had with him after my weekly Thursday night Mormon Tabernacle Choir rehearsals in Salt Lake City.

Not long after he finally underwent corrective surgery, genetic tests confirmed that our sweet baby did indeed have Down syndrome. It was something I had never imagined would be a part of my life. Jen and I already knew some of the challenges that came with being parents of a special-needs child, as our oldest son had an autism-spectrum learning disability. I realized Heavenly Father had once again sent us in an unexpected direction.

Over the next year, Bryson underwent a series of surgeries and procedures to correct various other birth defects. For many months, he could eat only out of a feeding tube inserted directly into his stomach, and there was a surgery both to insert the tube and eventually to close the hole. How to feed our baby was only one of many new skills we had to learn.

The initial coming to grips with the concept of raising a child with Down syndrome clouded my long-term perspective. I realized how little I knew about his condition and what his future might be like. As I tried to wrap my head around the concept, I often wondered why Bryson had to come to earth as he had, and Jen and I spent a lot of time in prayer.

Then one day as I prayed for peace, a wonderful thought came to my mind: *Bryson is going to heaven, and he wants to take you along.*

These words resonated deeply. I realized I didn't need to worry about him. He would influence many people for good, and because of his life, he would open doors to take many of those people along with him to his heavenly destination. Since then, I have been completely at peace with Bryson's condition.

At the time Bryson made his entrance into our lives, I had been out of a job for almost a year. This meant that when he was born, we were receiving help from Medicaid. To our relief, it took care of the majority of Bryson's six-figure medical bill. Still, because I had not been able to find employment despite my concerted effort, I had felt like a failure for a long time. Within a few months of Bryson's birth, I finally succeeded in finding an excellent job and went back to work full-time. It was then I realized what a great blessing I had been given—to be there to help my son and love him and to give support to my wife and our children during those long weeks of hospitalization. It was also a blessing later on to share with my wife the anxious hours of trying to care for a handicapped newborn baby.

Bryson is now a happy, healthy three-year-old toddler, and what I predicted the first time I saw him has come true in a wonderful way. I have never seen a child with such a loving personality, such a bright countenance, and such a joy for life. When we go out, our sweet son turns heads with his beaming grin and infectious laugh.

Every day seems like an incredible gift, and just being around him makes me want to be a better person. Others also naturally want to be kinder, gentler, and more loving when they are around him. We now can't imagine life without him, and we all agree that we never want to live anyplace where he is not with us. We hope to go with him to heaven.

Michael D. Young is a graduate of Brigham Young University and Western Governors University, with degrees in German, music, and instructional design. Though he grew up traveling the world with his military father, he now lives in Utah with his wife, Jen, and their two sons. He enjoys acting in community theater, performing and writing music, and writing both fiction and nonfiction. He played for several years with the hand-bell choir Bells on Temple Square and is currently a member of the Mormon Tabernacle Choir.

Have miracles ceased? Behold I say unto you, Nay; neither have angels ceased to minister unto the children of men.

—*Moroni 7:29*

WE WERE NOT ALONE
By Shauna Dalton

It was 1990 and my first year as girls camp director. We were living in Las Vegas, and our camp was about three hours away on Cedar Mountain, outside of Cedar City, Utah, at the Deer Haven campground. Our stake had chosen the earliest date possible to camp out with our girls, and the weather in Utah continued to be cool at the higher elevations. It was our custom to take the Mia Maids and Laurels on Saturday to set up camp, and the Beehives would join us on Monday.

During our week at camp, our ward was known as the "Crestwood Green Dragons." Every ward had a name and wore a colored bandana to match; our color was green. I loved every day of camp, and I never knew I could work so hard, put in such long hours, and get up and do it again the next day!

I was struck by the spiritual growth of the girls in our Young Women program. Two years earlier, we had had only six girls attend girls camp. A year later, the number grew to twelve, and this year almost thirty girls attended, along with their leaders. Excitement ran high, but we were in for a few challenges!

My first challenge came when the tread on one of the tires on my Jeep came off about twelve miles outside of Mesquite, Nevada. Thankfully, a priesthood leader followed us into Mesquite and stayed with us while we had a new tire put on, then made sure we were safely on the road again. We still made it up the mountain before the rest of our group finished unloading.

We arrived to find the sky dark and cloudy and the wind blowing hard. With one eye on the sky, everyone worked feverishly to get all the tents up before the rain started. Just as we finished, the first drops of rain fell. We were ready to run into our dry tents just as one more group arrived: sisters from the small Spanish branch in our stake. In the pouring rain, everyone ran over to help them put up all their tents.

It rained hard, and the wind blew steadily all Saturday night. A camp leader from another ward offered a special prayer for our camp and later related to us that as a child she had spent a lot of time riding horses with her grandfather in these mountains. She said when the wind came on these mountaintops, it often blew right through the trees, ripping them up and blowing them down without mercy. So this night she prayed, not for the wind to stop but for the wind to *rise to the top of the trees and not harm our camps.* And so the first miracle happened: the winds raged above us, and no harm came to us that night.

The next day, Sunday, the weather eased enough that we were able to hold sacrament meeting and a special YW program. It sprinkled, but it didn't dampen our spirits. After our meetings, stake priesthood leaders came to each camp and informed us that a tropical storm was brewing, uncommon for this time of year. We wondered if we should stay or tear down camp and go back to Las Vegas.

Our leaders knew of some cabins Church members owned, and they suggested we head there for now. Our stake president asked me how long it would take us to get ready, and I replied, "Fifteen minutes."

We were told to have each girl bring a sleeping bag—no blankets—a toothbrush, pajamas, and only snack food. We were to leave everything else behind. Because I had always been taught that we never question our priesthood leaders, I never gave it a second thought. I simply began organizing the girls. Then I found out one ward turned down the suggestion to move to the cabins, so one of my leaders and one my girls asked if they could stay behind too.

"It's all or nothing. Get your stuff together quickly," I told them.

I had three girls with me in my Jeep, plus a lot of supplies. As we were traveling up the narrow, muddy road, it was raining hard, and my windshield fogged up. Unfortunately, for the last two years, the defrost blower on my windshield had been broken, and though I had tried to repair it, it was to no avail. I could blow heat everywhere else but never on my windshield. Because of that and the drop straight down on the right side of the road, I prayed silently for protection and help.

I asked my daughter in the front seat to wipe the windshield off with a scarf, but it wasn't enough. I could not see where I was going, so I blindly followed the fading taillights in front of me. Feeling frantic,

I asked my daughter, who often drove the Jeep, to turn on the defrost fan. She knew it didn't work; however, she reached down and flipped the blower on anyway. To our surprise, it immediately came on and cleared the windshield in seconds.

Relief flooded through me. I realized the Lord was watching over and protecting us.

The cabins were wonderful! In the midst of a storm, we were snug. Our cabin housed thirty-five of us, and other campers went to three more cabins scattered in different directions.

The girls had a ball eating snack foods and staying up late braiding key chains and each other's hair. Before bed, our stake president invited us to join him in a family home evening.

The next morning, we were able to return to our camp. As we approached, we were amazed to see only one tent had blown down: the food tent. However, the canvas had protected all the food inside.

As we arrived, the one ward that had stayed behind was in the process of breaking camp. The storm had drenched them and most of their belongings. Everyone was cold and wet, and they were leaving to head down the mountain to Cedar City to find a Laundromat, where they could dry out everything. But they never returned.

To our delight, it never rained hard again, nor did the wind blow the rest of our time on the mountain. Those of us who had simply followed priesthood direction found ourselves dry and warm and excited to begin all our camp activities.

We held two testimony meetings that day. The first one was with the stake. The Beehive girls had arrived around noon, in time to take part in the stake's marvelous family home evening about Joseph Smith and the Savior and their sacrifices for us. Then we bore testimonies. We felt a sweet spirit as many girls stood to share their feelings, but there wasn't time for everyone to bear their testimonies. On the way back to our camp, one of our first-year girls asked if she had to bear her testimony. I told her she didn't need to bear her testimony unless the Spirit prompted her to.

It was after 10:00 p.m. when we returned to camp, but even so, I suggested we continue our testimony meeting with just our ward around our campfire. Some of the leaders thought the girls should go straight to bed, but as camp director, I felt strongly prompted that some of the girls needed more time and that we should continue.

Everyone huddled around the fire in blankets, and almost everyone bore their testimonies. Some actually bore testimony twice that night. The Spirit was very strong! And to my surprise, the young Beehive girl who had not wanted to participate stood in this more private setting and shared her thoughts with us. We finally closed with a prayer and sent everyone to bed.

Later, I walked through the camp, checking on all the girls. They were exhausted and had gone right to sleep. I stayed awake until midnight, talking with one of the Young Women leaders, a friend of mine. As we prepared to go to sleep, I decided to take one last look out our tent window.

I saw a bright light inside the Mia Maid tent, and three figures standing just outside, all dressed in white. I figured the girls had to use the restroom. We decided to give them about ten minutes and the benefit of the doubt. When I looked again, there was an extremely bright light coming from within the tent. I realized the zipper was unzipped, and I saw several white figures emerge from the tent and disappear into the dark. I didn't have my glasses on and couldn't see where they went, but I watched for what felt like a long time, and no one came back.

Now I was worried. Were my girls up to some kind of mischief? I found my glasses and put them on, then crawled out of my tent. A plan formed, sort of. I'd hide inside their tent, and when they came back, I'd surprise them. When I reached the tent, to my surprise, I found all the girls accounted for and sleeping soundly.

Silently I looked around to see if I could see anyone at all dressed in white. In the darkness, I could not catch a glimpse of them anywhere. I returned to my tent and discussed it with my friend. We both experienced an overwhelming and unmistakable feeling that we had had heavenly visitors, not only watching over us but also coming to check on us in person.

The next morning the girls assured us they had been too tired to pull any pranks, and no one had come to visit them in their tent. They had felt safe and peaceful all night.

We talked with some of the other camps about what we had seen and found out others had had a similar experience that night. We had truly been watched over!

I had other experiences later on that confirmed to me that personages had indeed been there, and I have often wondered why we were blessed to see those who had walked among us that night. Perhaps the extraordinarily sweet spirit we'd had among us around the campfire had in some way opened our eyes. Or maybe the great spirits of these very special girls under my care merited this experience in some way. Though I may never know in this life, I will always be grateful that I experienced it.

We moved from the ward and state a few years later and have lost track of many of the girls. However, of the girls I have been able to learn about, all have married and are raising wonderful families. They are scattered around the United States, including Alaska and Hawaii, but no matter where they are, I like to think angels are still watching over them.

Shauna Dalton and her husband have six children and twenty-one grandchildren. The couple served an inner-city mission to a ward in Salt Lake City and later decided to move into that ward. Recently the Daltons moved to Bella Vista, Arkansas. Shauna has served in many Church callings, including Relief Society president, teacher, and ward activities director.

They had given themselves to much prayer, and fasting; therefore they had the spirit . . . of revelation.

—Alma 17:3

A VERY UNPLEASANT ANSWER TO PRAYER

Name Withheld

When I was in junior high school, I absolutely hated going to P.E. It didn't matter what the game was, I got chosen last for every team, every year. The gymnasium was tiny, so boys took P.E. on Tuesdays and Thursdays, and girls took P.E. on Mondays and Wednesdays. On Fridays we met together and had dance lessons.

In Friday's class, there were two more girls enrolled than boys. Therefore, every boy had to ask a girl to dance for every dance. But that always left two girls to stand on the sidelines. Now besides being humiliated on every P.E. day, I also found myself one of the two girls who seldom got asked to dance on Fridays, so I took to praying over this inequality of numbers. *Just let me get asked to dance!* This prayer did not get answered with any regularity.

Somehow I survived junior high, but I never fooled myself that I was very pretty or fashionable or popular. I knew otherwise, and the lessons of junior high stayed with me as I moved on to college. Attending Brigham Young University did not improve things. In my last semester of college, I had exactly zero dates. Somehow I'd managed to get a BS without the accompanying MRS.

I moved to another state and began working. At long last a young man came into my life, and I had a strong impression that this was the man the Lord had been preparing for *me*. Really? I was so grateful when we married and settled down to have a large family.

The years passed, and I served faithfully in many Church callings. One day I was invited to visit with a member of the stake presidency and received a call to work in a stake position. This meant a great deal to me. I loved the gospel, and I looked forward to serving with all my heart, might, mind, and strength. One of the programs our stake organized needed ongoing support from the men of the high council, and every month we would get together, sometimes in meetings but more often at activities. I began making many friends throughout the stake, and for about three years, I worked hard and allowed myself to blossom under interesting challenges and assignments. Stake conferences became a time of greeting many, many friends—the girl who had always been chosen last warmed to the fire of so many friendships.

One high councilor stood out. He too worked hard and never missed a meeting. We often chatted informally while watching activities from the sidelines. I found him easy to talk to, and our friendship grew. We laughed together a lot and discussed many things as we enjoyed these fun times together.

I wondered if it was okay to be friendly like that. I couldn't see anything wrong, yet increasingly, whenever we found ourselves in the same room, we'd find ourselves walking toward each other like a couple of magnets. It was *always* fun to talk to him, but I continued to wonder. We never spoke on the phone, we never saw each other at any other time, there were always lots of people around, and nothing improper had *ever* been said or done. Still . . .

A year passed. One day I decided I needed to know just how friendly was okay with the Lord. Fast Sunday approached, and it seemed a good time to pray about it. After church I told my husband I needed a few minutes alone. He stayed home with the children, and I drove to a quiet place and prayed. Inside, I felt confused. I knew I had not done anything wrong, exactly, so why did I feel like I was doing something wrong? I truly desired enlightenment. Maybe a scripture would come to mind, I thought as I opened mine. Perhaps a gentle thought, a quote, a message from a conference talk. I was waiting to be sweetly taught.

Time passed. I needed to get back home and rescue my dear husband from the Sunday chaos. But I also needed an answer, so I sat in the car and thought about everything and then prayed again to understand. All at once, I felt a deep anger come through the veil! Then words came into my mind: *You are allowing Satan to use you to tempt members of the high council!*

Shock ran through me. Satan was *using* me? The first thought that came to mind was, *Gosh, he must be desperate.* The junior high school "me" found the concept quite impossible. Other than my wonderful husband, nobody had *ever* paid the least attention to me.

In that moment, I wanted comfort, forgiveness, and warmth from the Spirit, but it didn't come. I was in trouble, and my actions had not been pleasing to the Lord. I felt absolutely crushed inside for many reasons. I loved the Lord and had always tried hard to keep the commandments, so this really shook me to the core. I had not seen it coming, and it was definitely not the gentle teaching moment I had expected. No, I had been chastised.

Over the years, I had sat through endless lessons about resisting temptation, but I had never considered the fact that the adversary might be using me to tempt others. It was sobering to think about. And the message had been plural: *members* of the high council. I knew of no other person I had ever paid any particular attention to, so this confused me even more.

I made some rules for myself then and there.

At the next activity, my high councilor friend saw me and came over to say hi. I called him Brother and smiled, said a couple of words, then turned to speak to someone else. I moved away and made it a point to talk to everyone I could. That marked the beginning. I decided I would *never* encourage special friendships with anyone acting in a priesthood capacity no matter how many times our paths crossed in any given calling.

That was over twenty years ago, and to this day, I have never crossed that line. I later decided to extend that resolve to refrain from encouraging close friendships with *any* man who was not my husband.

I sometimes wonder what might have been the ending if I had not thought to fast and pray about a situation that seemed harmless in many ways yet troubled me at some level. While I did not like the answer I received, I knew I had done the right thing in asking. I know the Lord loves us and will help us understand situations that seem perplexing. How to keep every commandment and know where the Lord's boundaries are within the details of our daily routines can sometimes be hard to figure out, but I know now that He will enlighten us and guide us when our hearts are pure and we truly desire to know truth. Fasting brought needed insight I could not have obtained in any other way. When I really, really need answers, fasting allows me to go an extra mile, and when I do, I am taught that which is *most needful* for me to know, even if I do not like the answer.

WE FEEL HIS LOVE AS WE ARE GUIDED IN HOW TO SOLVE OUR PROBLEMS

Verily, verily, I say unto thee, blessed art thou for what thou hast done; for thou hast inquired of me, and behold, as often as thou hast inquired thou hast received instruction of my Spirit. If it had not been so, thou wouldst not have come to the place where thou art at this time.

—*D&C 6:14*

THE MESSAGE
Name Withheld

I had been married to my husband, a branch manager of a bank in our community, for about nine years. We led a happy life filled with vacations to Hawaii, a country club membership, boating weekends, and important community connections. Two years earlier, I had given birth to our precious daughter. Life was fabulous! So when my husband came to me one day and said, "I'm not happy," I was shocked. He continued. "I'm moving in with my parents to figure things out."

This was news to me. What could be wrong? Strange things began to take place. Our new routine took shape: he would come home after work, eat dinner, then go back to work at the bank until he went home to sleep at his parents' house. On Tuesdays he played basketball with his guy friends and didn't come home at all. Saturday nights he went out with friends without including me. He was gone a lot, but that was what successful men did. Or so I thought.

Then one day the phone rang. It was a Saturday night, and a woman's voice on the other end of the line said, "Where is your husband?" I recognized the voice as belonging to one of the tellers at the bank where my husband worked.

"He's with friends," I reluctantly replied.

"No, he's not," she replied. "He's right here. I'm at the Delta Center on a pay phone at a Jazz game, and he is walking up to me right now." Suddenly, the phone went dead.

A flood of emotions ran through my body, and I started shaking. I felt sick to my stomach, and I wanted to cry. Things I'd found puzzling started to make sense. Those long hours had most likely been spent not at work but with an attractive young woman!

Minutes later, the phone rang again, and the same voice said, "Why won't you sign the divorce papers?"

Shaking, I asked, "Where is my husband?"

"On his way home. Why won't you sign the divorce papers?" she repeated. "I have been in love with your husband for three years, and we want to get married."

"I don't know anything about divorce papers."

"Well, he showed them to me. Why won't you sign them?"

It was clear at this point that my husband had been conning both of us.

It seemed like hours until I heard the garage door open. What should I say? What excuses and lies would he come up with to justify his behavior? I immediately started asking questions, and he calmly reassured me that the woman was crazy and had made the whole thing up. He insisted she was nothing more than a troublemaker. He told me how much he loved me, and he assured me he would be moving back home soon. That was all I needed to hear. My world was not collapsing, and everything was going to be okay.

The following Monday night came, and this was going to be the test. Would he leave after we put our baby to bed? At nine, he left, telling me he was going to the bank to get in a few more hours of work. I looked up the number of the bank teller in the phone book and dialed. Her mother answered and acknowledged that her daughter was with my husband. I asked if she would have her call me when she got home, no matter the time. At eleven, the teller called and openly admitted she had been with my husband, *just like always.*

I invited her over, and we sat on the couch until four in the morning very calmly comparing notes about our shared relationship with my husband. The details stunned me. Their time spent together and the extent of their three-year affair, including intimacy, shocked me.

It was worse than I could have ever imagined.

At four in the morning, we called his parents' house and asked to speak with him. His mother called him to the phone, and when he picked up the extension, unbeknown to us, his mother stayed on the line and continued to listen.

I told him I knew he had been with his girlfriend, but he assured me he had not.

The girlfriend took the phone and exclaimed, "Yes, you *were* with me!" Dead silence. The next thing he said was, "I love you both!"

I heard no remorse in his voice whatsoever. The following day, his mother visited me and assured me she would talk to her son. But nothing came of their discussion.

In the meantime, I had landed in unfamiliar territory. My world was tilting, and I didn't know what to do to fix it. Should I walk out? Or should I make an effort to save the marriage? I felt I ought to try to save it. The fight was on.

We had been living a very worldly lifestyle, and with it had come inactivity in the Church. Although married in the temple, we no longer attended our Sunday meetings. I always felt guilty about not going to church, and now I felt like I needed God in my life to guide my decisions. I started to attend without my husband so I could take our daughter to Primary, and the day came when I consulted with my bishop about the events going on in my life. Because of my husband's infidelity, a church court convened. The bishop hoped this would prove to be a wake-up call to my husband, but my husband didn't bother to attend. He was excommunicated.

The day was dark and cloudy, both literally and emotionally. I felt sad for his soul. He had been a member of the Church his whole life but had strayed step by step away from his beliefs.

Part of me knew the time had come to move on, yet I continued to hold on to hope that this relationship could be repaired. We had a daughter to consider. I was praying for answers on whether to stay or move on when one Saturday morning I had a feeling that I should drive to a certain grocery store. I saw both my husband's and his girlfriend's cars parked side by side, but they were sitting close together in the back of his van. He was still lying to me.

During this time, I had started seeing a counselor, but after six months of meeting together, she had not convinced me to move on. I kept telling her she didn't understand. Later, I realized it was me who didn't understand. She finally gave up on me and sent me to another counselor, and when I told him my story, he said five words to me: "You are a kept woman."

Shock ran through me. I will never forget those words. He told me frankly that I was nothing more than a doormat, that my husband wiped his feet on me when he came in and when he went out. Those were the words I needed to hear.

At that point, I had lived alone with my daughter for over a year and a half, and one evening I knelt at my bedside and poured my heart out to the Lord. A glorious sight unfolded to my mind. I saw the room full of people. Couples were looking down at me with a look of pleading in their eyes. At first I thought they were sent to me to comfort me, that God was letting me know I had people, family members or guardian angels, watching over me on the other side to comfort me in this time of pain, but I didn't know why they had pleading looks on their faces.

Still, it seemed clear that I needed to proceed with the divorce. I needed a strategy. A friend and I discussed my exit plan. For two weeks I pretended that I believed everything my husband said, that I really trusted him when he said he wasn't seeing the other woman and that he would move home soon. He was so happy that I accepted his words and seemed willing to go forward on promises, but I knew that if I continued to play along, he would lead his double life indefinitely.

Two weeks later I met his girlfriend in the church parking lot, waiting for him while he played basketball inside.

"Have you been with my husband lately?" I asked.

"Yes," she said. They had been together just the night before.

That's all I needed to hear. "Let's go in and talk to him."

When he saw his wife and his girlfriend walk into the gym together, with all his buddies watching, he turned pale.

"Come with us. We need to talk to you!" his girlfriend called out.

He completely ignored us and continued playing basketball.

Finally, the girlfriend lost her temper. We all walked outside, my husband's girlfriend screaming at him. I remained silent. When she finished, I simply said, "I gave you one more chance, and you blew it." I walked to my car and drove home, where I had already changed the locks. He was served divorce papers the following Monday morning.

At first he balked. However, bank employees, neighbors, a florist who was sending flowers to both the girlfriend and me, family members, and customers of the bank watched the drama unfold. His father finally said, "Take her to lunch, give her anything she wants, and make this quiet and simple." That was what he finally did.

We agreed on alimony, child support, cash settlement, visitation, and division of assets. It was simple and quick, and I could get on with my life.

After I received my final divorce papers, I had a dream. In it, the girlfriend, my husband, and I were all in white, suspended as if we were standing on clouds. He was in the middle holding on to both of our hands, one on each side of him. We were both pleading for him to come with us. He was caught in the middle. He looked at me, then deliberately turned away and let go of my hand. He and the woman ran hand in hand away from me, downward. But when he released my hand, I began ascending upward toward the light.

When I woke up, I experienced a feeling of euphoria beyond words. *He was holding me down.* This dream validated my decision because I had been asking God, "Why do I have to get a divorce? Why can't You just fix this for me?" The dream made it perfectly clear where my husband was heading and where I needed to go.

Three years had passed since I'd discovered my husband's affair, and I had spent most of those years living in pain. It *was* time to move on with my life. But what did that mean?

I decided to go dancing at the Bay, a local disco for people thirty-five and older. That first night I noted a man standing alone against the wall, watching people dance. I thought he was handsome but wondered why he didn't dance.

One week later, I saw him again. This time I walked up to him and asked him why he didn't like to dance.

"I do like to dance. Do you want to dance with me?" he said.

We danced, and then he asked me out for the following Saturday.

Our relationship developed quickly. We had lots in common. Four months later we were engaged. I couldn't believe I had found Mr. Right so fast. Perhaps God was blessing my life because I had just gone through so much. Maybe it was my turn to be happy.

He proposed to me on Temple Square with the Christmas lights and the Christus statue visible in the window in front of us. He said he loved me and promised to bring me back there to be sealed someday.

I thought that was a wonderful plan, and, with tears in my eyes, I accepted his proposal. We made the announcement to our families, and everyone was happy for us.

A few weeks later I was awakened in the middle of the night. I sat up in bed as I became aware that I was not alone. I received a clear message that if I wanted a temple marriage, *I needed to be married there now!* I had one more chance to get it right.

This message came so clearly that I could not deny what I knew must happen. I had to tell my fiancé. We both had to be temple worthy and ready and start off our life together by marrying in the Lord's house. He was not happy. He walked out the door and drove away, and our engagement ended.

What had I done? I fell to the floor in tears. I didn't want to lose him, but I couldn't deny the message I'd received from a loving Heavenly Father. I *wanted* to get it right with God. I *needed* to get it right.

One morning I was in the kitchen doing the dishes and feeling a lot of emotional pain. As the sun was coming through the window, warm and comforting, an impression came to my mind. I could see those same people who had appeared to me in my bedroom a year earlier while I had been praying. Suddenly, I understood what their pleading faces meant. They were pleading with me to do their temple work! I knew they wanted me to become worthy of a temple recommend and hurry back to the temple so I could do their work for them. This experience confirmed to me that I needed to continue to work extremely hard to go to the temple. Their eternal salvation was in my hands; they were depending on me.

At a dance some months later, I ran into my ex-fiancé. He was with a twenty-something girl.

"Hi, Miss 'I *Do* Want to Get Married in the Temple.' What are you doing in a place like this?" he asked.

I was embarrassed and realized neither one of us should have been in a club like that. Plus, it was painful seeing him with someone else. I knew then how much I missed him and loved him.

He called me a few days later and said, "What are we doing? Would you like to go out on Friday?"

I couldn't say yes fast enough, so we went out Friday and then began dating again. We started attending church together for the next three months. Soon he announced that he was meeting with the bishop. We were careful to say good-bye at ten o'clock every night, and we began temple preparation classes.

By the time we got engaged a second time, we still had six months to wait. But the time went quickly. We became very spiritually connected because of the goal we were so diligently working toward. We became best friends with a very important mountain to climb together.

On the day we married, in May 1990, we felt on top of the world for many reasons. Most of all, we were happy because we had followed the counsel the Spirit had given me, and we knew God was pleased that we had worked so hard to make it happen.

My husband and I have now been married for twenty-four years. We have been blessed with six children between us and double blessed with ten grandchildren. We have served a two-year inner-city mission in North Salt Lake City, Utah; my husband has served for eight years as a veil worker in the Jordan River Temple; and I have served fourteen years as an ordinance worker. As I think of all those people who appeared to me in my time of pain, it puts a smile on my face. I know there is no longer pleading in their eyes. Now there is a warm smile of everlasting peace on their faces and eternal happiness in their hearts!

Yes, the journey seemed long, with many pain-filled moments, but I became aware during those years that the Spirit was seeking ways to help me turn my life toward the things of the Lord. I am grateful for this knowledge that God loves us and will help us make whatever changes we need to so we can partake of the happiness and blessings that living the gospel brings.

Verily I say unto you, Inasmuch as ye have done it unto one of the least of these my brethren, ye have done it unto me.

—*Matthew 25:40*

$\mathscr{S}$AVING CASSI
By Jessica Nelson

During the summer of 2004, I had the wonderful privilege of working as a girls camp counselor at the LDS Oakcrest Girls Camp in Kamas, Utah. As a counselor, I was responsible each week to oversee a new group of girls, thirteen and fourteen years old, who came from different stakes in the Salt Lake Valley and the surrounding areas. Our staff of fifty-five had lots of great things planned for the girls.

The day before the girls arrived, all the counselors were given a list of the young women who would join their group for that week. My first week, as I looked over the names on my list, I became concerned because some of the girls had brightly colored sticky tabs next to their names. This meant they were girls with disabilities, allergies, or other ailments that we as counselors had to watch out for.

One girl's name stood out right away: Cassi. Next to her name, a lengthy list of allergies and illnesses had been written down and highlighted in pink. Among other things, this girl was allergic to bee stings, and she suffered from severe asthma. *Oh great!* I thought. *What is this girl doing here? This is the outdoors, there are bees everywhere, and we will be doing plenty of hiking and walking this week, which might trigger an asthma attack.*

Nevertheless, I accepted my list of girls with a prayer in my heart and hoped everything would turn out all right. I was comforted by the thought that because this was our first week on the job, I would not be the only counselor with concerns about my list of girls. There were thirty other counselors, and surely a few of them would also be going through the same type of anxiety.

As soon as I met Cassi, I made sure to remember what she looked like so if anything alarming happened, I could quickly help. Cassi was a petite five foot three, had blonde hair and blue eyes, and weighed no more than 115 pounds. At first glance, she looked healthy, but looks can be deceiving.

The first couple of days went well, and I got along fine with the girls without any notable problems. I began to feel more at ease. On Wednesday, we were scheduled to go on an overnight hike with our girls. We gathered our camping supplies and headed up the mountain to the campground. The hike wasn't very long, and when we arrived at the campsite, I was paired with another counselor, Stephanie, and her girls for the night.

Our campsite included a large blue tarp tied to four trees—it was the only source of shade we had. While our girls laid out their sleeping bags, my fellow counselor and I began to gather wood for the campfire so we could get dinner started in our dutch oven. We had scarcely started the fire and put the dutch-oven meal on to cook when I received the strongest prompting—a warning. Something was going to happen very soon, and I needed to be prepared for it so I could handle it the right way.

This feeling was so strong that it gave me the chills. I had never received such a clear prompting before, so it threw me into a panic because I had no idea what to prepare for. I tried my best to keep it together and think clearly. Then I had a feeling that I should speak to Stephanie about the impression I had received. When I told her, she said she'd had the exact same impression but she didn't know what to do about it or how to prepare for it either. We decided not to say anything to the girls, but we said a quiet prayer before continuing our dinner preparations. We became ever watchful of the girls and our surroundings.

I wondered what might go wrong: a bear or a moose attack? Rain? Injury? The list went on and on in my head. What should I prepare to cope with? Soon after, as I was sitting on a fallen log by the campfire, I saw a huge bumblebee buzzing around. It landed on a flower right in front of me.

Immediately, Cassi came to mind. So strong was my feeling that she should be the focus of our preparations that I approached Stephanie and shared my concern with her. We both got up quietly and walked over to check on Cassi, who was lying on her sleeping bag, exhausted from the hike. I asked her how she was feeling. She gave me a puzzled look and said she was fine, just a little tired and hot. After hearing she was fine, I breathed a sigh of relief and calmed down.

If Cassi was fine, why had I been given such a specific and distinct prompting? I kept a close eye on her just in case. About ten minutes later, she came up to me and asked for her inhaler. She explained that she was having a hard time breathing. I ran to my bag, grabbed the inhaler, and gave it to her. She put it into her mouth and inhaled the medicine with a few deep breaths, but it didn't help, so she tried it again and again. When she didn't improve, she started to panic and cry hysterically. She struggled to breathe, and her hands began to shake. She was having a severe asthma attack, and the inhaler wasn't working.

That was when Stephanie, who was both taller and stronger than I was, grabbed Cassi in a cradle hold and began to run as fast as she could back to the main campsite. I stayed behind to take care of the rest of the girls.

Fortunately, I had the two-way radio on me. I called the camp director at the main campsite and told her to prepare for an emergency. Cassi would be there soon and needed immediate transportation to the nearest hospital. When Stephanie arrived at the main campsite with Cassi in her arms, our camp director was waiting and prepared. They rushed Cassi to a nearby hospital in Heber City. By the time she arrived, due to a lack of oxygen, Cassi's hands were turning blue, but emergency room nurses quickly stabilized her, and a few short hours later, she returned to camp.

Because of the promptings we both felt, Stephanie and I acted immediately to help this sweet young girl. If we had hesitated or underrated the danger, as we certainly might have done otherwise, things could have turned out far worse. I will always thank Heavenly Father for preparing us for this situation so we could give quick help in a time of need.

Jessica Nelson was born in Perm, Russia. At the age of twelve, she was adopted by an American family in Utah, where she grew up. Jessica is married to Seth Nelson, and they are parents of two sweet little girls, Seraphim and Angelica. Currently the family resides in Murray, Utah.

Blessed is the man that trusteth in the Lord, and whose hope the Lord is. For he shall be as a tree planted by the waters, and that spreadeth out her roots by the river, and . . . her leaf shall be green.

—Jeremiah 17:7–8

WAITING FOR A MIRACLE
By William Kay Randall & Renee Grow

Bill:

I was born and raised in the dusty little town of Winslow, Arizona. Most people consider small towns pure boredom, but looking back, growing up in Winslow was pure adventure, and I didn't leave that small heaven for little boys until I attended Brigham Young University. After five years of college, I married and took a job teaching elementary school, which I did for the next thirty years.

During that time, my wife, Shauna, and I raised four children, which was no easy task, and by the time I reached my forties, I was overweight and saddled with type II diabetes. In retrospect, I guess that was why some people referred to me as Sweet William. Diabetes was a horrible disease in and of itself, but the other maladies that tagged along with it were ongoing nightmares.

I was also diagnosed with acute liver disease that would end my life if I didn't do something about it fast. My doctor put me on a critical wait list with Intermountain Health Care in Utah for a liver transplant, and I began carrying a beeper with me twenty-four hours a day, hoping and praying for that miracle beep that would tell me I would have a chance at prolonging my life.

One day my beeper went off, and I received the call to hurry to the hospital! While Shauna drove like a racecar driver to get me to the operating room on time, I gulped down pills I had been instructed to take if the beeper should go off. When we arrived, the medical team was already assembled. I became aware that the potential donor was still alive—barely—and that his family had agreed to donate his organs. He was Hispanic, but that was all I was ever told. I prayed for him and asked the Lord to bless this man for his gift to me.

Everything became a blur as I was prepped for surgery. I fervently prayed and asked the Lord if I might have a guardian angel watch over me. Then I was taken into surgery.

The operation was successful. My recovery from the liver transplant went well, but when I was in my fifties, I started having trouble with my kidneys. The doctors who monitored my recovery informed me that the medications I had to take for the new liver were slowly killing my kidneys. Over a period of time, my kidney function continued to deteriorate. I was in my late sixties when the day finally came that I was placed on dialysis, with a tube inserted into my left arm, and I had to go to a dialysis center for ongoing treatment. Once again I was placed on a donor wait list, this time for a kidney transplant. The average wait time for a kidney match could be several years and depended on many factors, but the cut-off age was seventy, so I had only a small window of opportunity and little hope to go on.

Meanwhile, I had to undergo long hours of dialysis. Sitting in a chair with a machine pumping my blood to clean it was not a high point in my life. As I had little hope for a rescue, I fell into depression. I went to dialysis three times a week, and since I had about four hours to sit in a chair, I decided to write in my journal and bring my life history up to date. At church I bore my testimony frequently, nearly every fast Sunday, and I told ward members how much I loved my wife and family, loved the Lord, and loved them. I told them I was writing my life story and making other efforts to use this time of my life well, and many people from the ward offered love and support in many ways, including adding me to their fast each month.

About a year went by, and it was clear to everyone that I didn't have a lot of time left. I was low on the donor priority list, and I was running out of hope.

Renee:

My family and I had known the Randalls as ward members for many years. We also had another connection: we frequently ran into Bill at the Dimple Dell Recreation Center in Sandy, Utah, where he and Shauna, his wife, often went for swimming exercise and where my family went for various workouts. In particular, my teenage son Christian and my husband, Kevin, did many early-morning basketball workouts there. On many occasions, Bill would pop his head into the gym to visit and to watch Christian's progress. On a few occasions, he would even challenge Christian to a one-on-one, and they both had a great time trying to outplay each other.

That was Bill's personality to a T—always friendly and outgoing, even with the younger generation. We thought highly of him, so it was difficult watching his decline. Then one day we received sobering news. We had just finished attending a basketball tournament in San Francisco, California, and had a long, twelve-hour drive to Utah ahead of us. We left early and were on the road when I received a call from my sister Roxanne. She had just been informed that our strong and husky fifty-two-year-old brother, Raleigh, who lived in Hawaii, had fallen and hit his head. He had somehow made it back to his home and spoken to a roommate but almost at once collapsed after that. He was taken to the hospital, and because he had been what the staff called "combative," he was put under to keep him calm. Roxanne said she would keep us updated on his condition during our drive home.

I had been born and raised in Hawaii in a large family, but five of us now lived in Utah. My mother, a wonderful, single, divorced woman who raised us on her own, had died years ago, so it suddenly became the responsibility of the three oldest sisters, Shelley, Roxanne, and me, to make decisions for our brother. Various members of the extended family who still lived in Hawaii visited Raleigh by turn and called with updates, so we received ongoing reports of his progress during our trip home. Initially, it appeared he was doing okay. Once home, we were informed that the doctors had called in a specialist, and after additional tests, including an MRI, they found blood on his brain, which was not a good sign.

Then we received a call from the specialist. We were told that Raleigh would likely never regain any brain function and would live in a vegetative state for the rest of his life and need constant care. He asked if the family wanted to continue life support. The suddenness of this change in our brother's condition hit us hard. Raleigh, at this point in his life, looked like a healthy, typical Hawaiian man. This couldn't be happening.

As sisters, we knew one thing for sure: Raleigh would not want to continue to live on life support. It was with great sadness that we agreed we needed to let him go. We talked to the doctors in Hawaii and approved his removal from life-support systems.

Almost immediately, we received an unexpected call from an organization called Legacy of Life, Hawaii. A woman kindly explained their program of giving life, sight, and hope to others on waiting lists for organ donations. Would we consider allowing our brother to help others?

The darkness and sadness that had enveloped us for hours suddenly opened to a small pinprick of light. Could Raleigh's misfortune be turned into something good? He had been a very giving and humble man his whole life, and we knew he would want to do this. We agreed to donate his organs: eyes, liver, kidney, various tissues—the list was long. The next question took me by surprise. Did we know anyone currently on a waiting list for an organ donation whom we would like to help? We were told we had the right to direct the organs to whomever we wished.

In the midst of many tender feelings filling my heart and mind over the loss of my brother, Bill Randall's name came suddenly and clearly to mind. "Yes!" I said. "Bill Randall! He goes to my church and lives in my neighborhood in Sandy, Utah!" I asked permission from my sisters, Shelley and Roxanne, and they wholeheartedly agreed. It was a bittersweet moment for us.

In Hawaii, the woman quickly asked me for some information about Bill. She needed his birth date and asked that I call him. I quickly called him and asked for his pertinent information without giving a lot of details. I was excited to think that this might really help him, but at the same time, I worried that if the kidney wasn't a match, it could further dash his hopes. I called the woman at Legacy of Life and gave her the information she needed to continue the process of the kidney match for Bill. She said she would be in touch.

I thought it was probably a long shot that Raleigh's kidney could be a match for Bill, but it was worth a try. *What are the odds?* I wondered. It had been a long, eventful day, and my sisters and I were emotionally drained. With nothing else left to do in the late hours of the night, I went to bed.

Bill:

After talking to Renee, hope surged. It was wonderful to know she'd thought of me, but I knew that matches rarely happened that way. We went to bed wondering if anything would come of it.

The phone call came at 2:00 a.m., and I was told a kidney had become available and that I should prepare for a possible transplant. I was so excited I couldn't go back to sleep. I only knew that the donor was a Hawaiian man, and it would take hours to get the kidney here. They did not reveal his identity. At this point, I didn't know it was Renee's brother, and the hope that surged put all else out of my mind.

The fact that I had been called at all meant many things: First, someone, a stranger to me, was dying. But more than that, somehow the impossible had happened. Against all odds, a kidney had become available that matched the first two important milestones: blood type and genetic markers on white blood cells. Final tests would be done once the kidney arrived.

I was told to come to the hospital in the morning. Just before leaving for the hospital, I received another call, this one from Renee. She told me about her brother passing away in Hawaii, that his kidneys had been donated, and that she and her family had directed that if the kidney matched, it should come to me. My wife and I shed tears together. I no longer felt my donor was a stranger.

When the kidney arrived, I was waiting in the hospital. Final tests were done, and we waited anxiously for the results. Would it match?

It did! It was a perfect match.

Renee:

The next morning I woke up to the sad reality that I had lost my brother. And I learned that after I hung up with the woman from Legacy of Life the night before, things had started to happen very fast. Bill had evidently passed the initial factors for a match, so the kidney had quickly been loaded on an aircraft headed for Utah. Once it arrived, he had undergone more tests. I didn't know the results and only hoped for the best.

Then my youngest sister, Pualani, who was also a member of our ward, sent me a text message that read, "Did you see the e-mail from the Relief Society president?" I quickly looked at my e-mail and saw this:

Dear Sisters,

Great News!!! It's a go!!! Bill passed the heart tests and will receive a kidney transplant in the morning. Keep him in your prayers!! YEAH!!!!!!

Love, Susanne.

I quickly called my sisters. Then I called Bill.

Bill:

Word spread quickly throughout the ward that I had been given a kidney. The operation proceeded without any complications, and I found out later that the new kidney began working before I even left the operating room! God and His angels were watching over all of us.

Renee:

Before leaving to attend Raleigh's funeral in Hawaii, Shelley, Pualani, and I visited Bill in the hospital. To see his smiling face and know the kidney worked perfectly helped ease the pain of saying good-bye to our brother. Every time I see Bill, it warms my heart to think that this sweet man is alive and well and that we will always have a special connection to each other because of Raleigh's kidney. I don't know who else received organ transplants from Raleigh, but I do know Heavenly Father *knew* Raleigh and Bill and knew Raleigh's kidney would be a perfect match for Bill.

Bill:

Soon after the operation, I began receiving many visitors. Once home, there was a parade of people bringing food and cheer. This wonderful, amazing story of one ward member helping another brought great rejoicing from everyone. I was deeply grateful to be able to thank Renee and her family in person.

I know there is a loving God in heaven and that we are surrounded by His love and His wonderful angels, both on earth and in heaven. Miracles do happen in this world. I am walking proof of that. Coincidentally, I have also developed a real love of Mexican food, from my Hispanic liver donor, and now of pineapples as well! I feel a special kinship with the two people who gave me a new gift of life, and one day I know I will see them and thank them in person too.

William Kay Randall lives in Sandy, Utah, and is a retired elementary school teacher. He and his wife, Shauna, have four children and three grandchildren. Shauna makes quilts and often gives them away to the fire stations for use during emergencies, and Bill works in his leather-craft shop, making fly cases, belts, guitar straps, and other fun things. They enjoy family activities and being with grandchildren.

Renee Grow also lives in Sandy, Utah. She and her husband, Kevin, have three children and three grandchildren. Renee and Kevin have spent their free time in many capacities having to do with their children's interests, which include ballroom dancing, softball, and basketball. They are both presently serving in the Young Women and Young Men presidencies in their ward. Renee and Kevin have been blessed by the influence of many great friends and family, as well as by their ward family, who has shaped their lives for the better.

Seek not for riches but for wisdom; and, behold, the mysteries of God shall be unfolded unto you, and then shall you be made rich. Behold, he that hath eternal life is rich.

—D&C 11:7

$\mathscr{L}$EARNING SPIRITUAL LESSONS

By Elinor G. Hyde

Although I had a testimony of the gospel of Jesus Christ, recognizing spiritual promptings and answers to prayer took longer for me to understand than other gospel principles. Even so, some of the first important lessons I learned about communicating with God came while I was in my late teens.

One particular lesson came while in high school. I was on a baton-twirling team, and following our half-time performance for the Idaho State basketball tournament, our team was relaxing on the bleachers of the empty Pocatello High School auditorium. Our bus would not leave for several hours.

"Let's go to the girls' locker room," one of the girls suggested.

For some reason, I felt *very* uncomfortable about this, and I was glad when others countered the suggestion. "What would we do in there?" someone asked.

"I don't know. It can't be any less interesting than just sitting here."

We laughed and chatted awhile, then we sauntered over to the gym area, where a grim security guard stood at the locker room door. We discovered it had been rifled and many personal items had gone missing. We were firmly told to leave. Had we arrived even minutes earlier, we would have been very suspect.

From then on, I set a new guideline: if something didn't feel right, I would speak up. It was one of my first lessons in understanding how the Spirit can guide us.

My next experiences occurred while I was attending Brigham Young University. I signed up for an accounting class, something my father often urged but that I didn't want to do, and soon after classes began, I wondered why I was there. Nothing I studied made sense. I attended all my labs and sought tutoring from fellow students, but none of it helped much. Each class involved pieces of paper representing "books" labeled *Accounts Receivable, Accounts Payable, Inventory, Profit and Loss, Journal,* and others. I was glad I had other skills, including secretarial training and journalism aptitudes.

Alan, a new Canadian friend who I was casually dating, encouraged me to stick with my accounting class. I liked having guy friends as well as girl friends at college, especially Alan, since he'd made it clear his only interest in me was to have a friend to go places with without the complications of a potential romance waiting to develop. Since I had long-range "someday" plans with a young man in Idaho, this suited me just fine. My young man was currently preparing to become a missionary, and knowing there would be a long wait, I had entered college. Alan's words of encouragement helped me as I muddled through this difficult course.

Frequent reminders for students to ask for spiritual help, especially if we'd done our assignments and attended classes, didn't seem to make any difference with my accounting course. The final proved even worse than I'd anticipated. The last question counted as forty points, and I didn't even have time to start it. I prayed that the Lord would help me do the very best I could because I hadn't even comprehended important parts of the coursework, and I was fairly sure my best was not half good enough.

I was in for a huge surprise. Instead of a failing grade, I received a C for the class! How could that be? The professor had stressed often that he did not give Ds, since we "either knew the basics or we didn't." I didn't try to second-guess his judgment, but I did feel I'd been greatly blessed. I knew I had done the very best I could on the final, and my best, though not spectacular, got me a passing grade—a miracle. In truth, it was really only part one of a larger lesson.

Later on, I signed up to take a missionary class, but I had no idea it would entail so much work. I had hundreds of scriptures to memorize plus many assignments requiring that I prepare missionary discussions on various points. I didn't have a clue where to start.

Alan's gospel maturity proved very helpful as I worked on writing discussions and memorizing scriptures, which were difficult. However,

Alan seldom failed to astonish me. It seemed there was a scriptural answer to everything, and his constant backing kept me afloat.

As my finals approached, my concern turned monumental. I had to write at least 125 scriptures, with documentation, just to pass. Hearing one student rehearsing scriptures under exact subjects—the Godhead, premortal life, baptism, and so on—really upset me. I had simply memorized several each day as I'd come and gone. A feeling of desperation overwhelmed me. How could I possibly compete? *Please let me pass*, I prayed silently. *Just let me pass.*

As I began writing, scripture after scripture came to mind, and I felt an overwhelming surge of pure knowledge. For each one I wrote, three or four others came to mind. I thought, smugly, *I must know three hundred or more. Oh, will the class be mad at me!* Then, as I wrote my ninetieth verse, my mind went blank. I suddenly could not think of anything. This surely wasn't fair.

Quietly, I was reminded I'd prayed to *pass.*

I did pass—barely. The C was not what I'd expected but what I deserved. With my previous accounting class, I'd prayed to do my best . . . and it had been enough. Now I had prayed to *pass*, and that was all I'd done. Part two of the lesson hit me deeply. The Lord had given me just what I'd asked for both times! It was a sobering and severe lesson: pray for *specific needs.*

More lessons in spiritual understanding waited.

I had to attend a wedding, so I remained on campus during the break between two quarters. Alan invited me to the cafeteria for Sunday dinner, and we spent a comfortable time together. I shared my concerns over attending the upcoming wedding—one I'd been sorry to find out would not take place in the temple. Alan spoke of tender feelings toward his own family, some of whom had challenges with living gospel standards, and of his hope that he could one day help them. His compassionate response to my concerns impressed me. One seldom found a friend who communicated as he did.

During the following quarter, we both had busy schedules, but our paths still crossed frequently. We communicated well and enjoyed one another's company. When a gaudy advertisement for diamond rings arrived in the mail one day, my roommates and I put it on our door with our choices marked and a big note that read, "Let no man enter who is not rich." Alan wrote beneath it, "Seek not for riches but for wisdom; and, behold, the mysteries of God shall be unfolded unto you, and then shall you be made rich. Behold, he that hath eternal life is rich. D&C 11:7."

My roommates loved this and immediately adopted him as a big brother. I, on the other hand, began to realize he had changed his own rules and seemed ready to take our relationship to a deeper level. This put me in a difficult spot. Since we had agreed to be only good friends, I had not mentioned the underttstanding I had with the boy back home. Now, suddenly, I felt guilty about not telling him about the young man. It was not my nature to be deceitful, so in light of the new direction we had suddenly taken, every day I delayed telling him made me feel worse.

Finally, the truth came out, and as expected, it wasn't pretty. Alan had been very up front about girls who had once been important in his life. Why hadn't I been equally honest?

As my social life came to a screeching halt, my schoolwork suffered. Emotional turmoil filled my days. The worst part was knowing I had inflicted undeserved pain on a person who had been kind and good to me. Before long, however, Alan called a truce.

"I've always been the good guy and bowed out, but I've decided I'm here, and he's not, so we'll just exercise faith and see what happens." That solved the loneliness and pain, but now there was the young man at home to consider. He also deserved truthfulness.

Some days were good, and others were not, but Alan and I talked openly, even when I became cross and touchy. Perhaps subconsciously I hoped that if I was unpleasant enough, he would get tired of me and the problems would all just go away. Then one spring day, after spending hours at my sewing lab and wondering if I'd ever feel happy again, I glanced at the clock and realized I had put in more than enough time for the entire week. More importantly, I actually felt good! My emotional roller coaster seemed to have stopped for the moment. It was such a relief, and I enjoyed the walk back to the dorm.

I greeted Alan kindly when he came as usual to escort my roommates and me to Mutual. He seemed surprised at my new peace of mind and quietly said, "I wondered if you might be different."

Later, when we had a bit of privacy, I asked about his earlier remark. He carefully related his experience of returning with great sadness to his dorm and his anguished prayer about what to do. He told me he had received a powerful confirmation that all would be okay and to exercise patience. He then asked that I be given a witness as well. Most important, his prayer and my sudden realization that my tension was gone had happened at the very same time.

We said good night, promising to just let the situation play out until finals were over. Although the crushing weight of what to do about the missionary-to-be at home sometimes still intruded, I had to do my best to deal with what life was handing me.

As finals approached, I chose to study alone at the dorm one night, but I was interrupted by a dreadful scene between two roommates that escalated to a screaming climax. I stepped between them and received the full brunt of their anger as one slapped me. It shocked all of us, and their screaming stopped abruptly. But in my case, all my pent-up emotions surfaced, and I became hysterical and started to cry . . . and cry . . . and cry. In my entire life, I'd never experienced such distress.

Mercifully, everyone left me alone until a knock came at our door. To my embarrassment and, yes, complete amazement, Alan stood there. He quietly took me outside to a borrowed car, where we could talk. Earlier, while studying at the library, he'd experienced an overwhelming feeling that he needed to see me at once. The impression had come with such urgency that he had asked his best buddy for his car keys, and without question, the request had been granted.

That private hour proved to be precious. Mostly, Alan spoke gentle, kind words that included an open-ended proposal. The gist went something like this: *I don't want an answer now, but I want you to know just how I feel. I know you have a big decision to make, and I'm praying it includes me. We'll see what happens during our summer apart, and if we still feel the same come fall, we'll make this official.*

Peace swept over me. For my part, I *knew* that meant a Dear John letter would go into the mail the next day, finals or not. We added fasting to our prayers, asking that my letter would convey the right spirit. The letter would arrive only a few days before this young man's farewell and the end of school. I didn't want to bring a negative note into his wonderful event.

I had been back in Idaho for maybe fifteen minutes when my soon-to-be-missionary friend called to ask if we could talk. He arrived at our home about twenty minutes later. I expected a tough emotional scene, but instead, he told me that just a few nights earlier, he had dreamed that I came to him and told him I was in love with someone else. When he awoke, he thought, *Wow! That was pretty real.* My letter arrived that day.

He then confided in me that there was another girl who wanted to keep in touch with him while he served, and now he felt free to encourage her to write. Her family had already welcomed him in and loved him. As we talked about our experiences that had brought us to this moment, good feelings flowed between us. It was comforting to know he would have emotional support during his mission. I'd been released by being replaced. I truly felt a burden lifted.

Alan and I decided we would get married the following summer. I stayed in school until March, and we were married in June. Alan graduated the following August. And to my utter amazement, I found a job working at a tire company, doing bookkeeping! I warned the employer up front about my less-than-spectacular grade in accounting, but I was hired anyway. Within a couple of days, I suddenly understood "the books." I still thank my dad for insisting that I learn bookkeeping.

These experiences—first in high school and later in college—set my feet firmly on a road of spiritual awareness. I learned to heed feelings of unease, pray for outcomes most helpful and desirable, and recognize that inner peace is a sign that I am heading in the right direction. I am grateful for spiritual lessons learned during my school years because they enriched my learning far beyond academics.

Elinor G. Hyde is an author of prize-winning essays, stories, and articles. She has also published a novel, Canadian Windsong, *as well as many newsletters, historical sketches, and poems. Elinor has been married for fifty-nine years to Alan A. Hyde. They have six children, twenty-four grandchildren, and twenty-three great-grandchildren. They currently serve as stake historians.*

If any man thirst, let him come unto me, and drink.

—John 7:37

$\mathscr{O}$T WAS ALL TRUE!
By Linda Collins

I was raised Catholic and brought up in a military family. I had four sisters and a brother, and our father ruled with the fear of a belt. During my final year of high school, we were stationed in San Diego, and when I graduated, my father told me I had to move out on my own.

I panicked at the thought. I was only eighteen and didn't know how to budget. I couldn't drive, and I knew little of how to manage in the adult world. I had been dating someone for about a year, and when I told him I had to move out, he proposed marriage. I accepted, and it never entered my head that I might be compounding one problem with another.

I didn't think my parents, especially my father, would approve of my boyfriend. To pull off the marriage, I decided to lie. I told my parents I was pregnant, and my boyfriend and I eloped. I thought they would be furious, but they weren't. I think they were actually happy I'd left.

What should have been a time of elation in my life fast became the beginning of a series of one mistake after another. Of course, I truly got pregnant after the marriage. We both worked, but we were two naive kids totally unprepared for what was to come.

The insurance my husband had with his work supported what amounted to a maternity clinic. Whoever was on call examined me, but no single doctor followed my pregnancy. I was working and taking some college classes, and nine months came and went. Then ten months. I had gained fifty-six pounds on my puny little ninety-eight-pound frame. I didn't know what questions to ask and knew nothing about what to expect. They measured me and gave me every explanation in the book as to when to expect this baby. I sensed something was wrong. The doctors X-rayed me every week, but no one seemed to want to make a decision. I think they were passing me off, hoping the next doctor would deal with it. Eleven months went by. Finally, in my twelfth month, I went into labor.

After forty-eight hours in hard labor, I was taken to the delivery room and given something to help things along. I was exhausted, and the baby just wasn't coming. Finally, someone told me the baby was caught in the birth canal.

The doctor leaned into me and said, "You've got to give this everything you've got, and when I tell you to push, you have to give it *everything*."

I knew he meant business. Moments later, the baby came. The doctor said she was a good sixteen pounds! I must have passed out because my spirit left my body, and I observed everything that happened next from somewhere close to the ceiling of the delivery room.

I watched the team working on my daughter. She was blue as blue could be. They pumped oxygen into her and worked frantically to bring her around. Another team was positioned over me. Oxygen was being pumped into me too, and people were scrambling to bring me back. However, I found myself in the most beautiful and peaceful place anyone could imagine, and there weren't words in our language to express the peace and love I felt. Knowledge seemed to pour into me, including the fact that I had to go back. I didn't want to. I wanted to stay where I was.

I woke up in a hospital ward to my husband sitting by my bedside shocked and crying. He told me I was as white as the sheets. I felt so weak that I couldn't talk much, and I really didn't want to anyway. I didn't want to discuss what had happened because I truly had no words to describe it. I also found out I couldn't walk because my pelvic bones broke with the birth. I was a mess, and there were many rough roads ahead. One challenge was that because of the complications I had experienced, the doctor believed I would probably never be able to have more children.

For the time being, I just wanted to know where my baby was. I learned she had been put in one of the baby baskets, covered with a cloth so no one could see her, and pushed against the back wall. A priest came in to administer last rights because no one thought she had a chance of making it.

When they let me pick her up, I learned she was epileptic and had cerebral palsy and that there was the possibility of a few other problems as well. I held her and rocked her and loved her. It was the beginning of a very long road to recovery marked by precise instructions on medication, splints on her legs, and many, many frightening visits to the doctor. I was just thankful she was alive. Everyone commented about how she was the best baby, always smiling, and I was so thankful.

Sometime after that, my husband turned to alcohol. Life assumed a whole new perspective for me. I learned to go to my Heavenly Father for everything. There were times I thought I was being punished for the choices I had made—lying to my parents and then eloping. As ashamed as I am to say it now, there were times I contemplated taking my life. I would go into my closet, sit on the floor, and pray. Depression filled my life daily. Alcoholism was a terrible thing. Even the good times could be bad because of the alcohol in our home.

To my surprise, I got pregnant again. And again I had problems. Once more I went weeks over my due date, but this child, a lovely girl, was born healthy. By then the alcoholism had created so many problems that my husband and I divorced. I could not have foreseen in those difficult days that that would finally bring something good into my life.

I was left to raise the girls alone. I went to work in the field of sales, first selling cars and then insurance. One day I was asked to train a man with a young family. His name was Dave, and he spent time with me, driving around and helping with appointments. He learned a lot about me and my situation, my religion, and my family.

One day we were talking about religion, and I told him about this phenomenon on the news about a chapel in the middle of the poorest part of town that had had an image of the Virgin Mary appear in its window. People from all over the world were coming to see it. My mom had been begging me to take her, and I had set aside that very evening to do just that.

The next morning Dave asked me about our experience. I told him that Mom and I were so impressed! My mother was so moved by the experience that she cried. It was stirring to see the crowds and feel how spiritual the experience was.

Dave started to laugh.

I immediately felt insulted and angry. I learned he was a returned LDS missionary, and he began talking to me about his church. He talked so much about the LDS Church that I eventually asked him to just shut up. I was happy with my religion.

I got exactly what I asked for, and he shut up. He said no more to me about anything. I didn't know how long we'd ridden around together in this irritating silence, but it finally got to me. I asked him to talk, talk about anything, just talk.

He spoke about living prophets and how they guide us today just like in the days of Moses. He invited me to hear a prophet speak, to go with him and his wife to hear Spencer W. Kimball, who was coming to Balboa Stadium to speak. I didn't know why, but I accepted.

Oh my gosh! *Oh my gosh!* Everything I had learned in my out-of-body experience after my first daughter's birth came back as I listened to Spencer W. Kimball! It was all true. *God lived.* He heard and answered prayers. I was home. *I knew I was home.* I followed the prophet everywhere he spoke on that trip to San Diego just so I could hear him. I was in heaven.

Dave and his wife invited me to dinner at their home, and I accepted. I didn't know the missionaries were going to be there, but they were, and I heard the first lesson. Of course, they asked if I'd like to know more, and I responded affirmatively. They told me I didn't live in their area so they would have to give my name to elders who could teach me. I waited and waited, but no one came. I was really discouraged.

One day I was driving home from work and happened to see missionaries on their bikes in front of me. I cut them off with my car, jumped out, and shouted, "Where have you been?" Startled, they asked, "Who are you?"

I proceeded to give them my information, and again I was told they did not teach in my area.

"We'll make sure someone contacts you right away."

That time I received missionaries quickly, and my journey moved forward with praises to the Lord for His gospel and for saving my life.

I was so elated to hear the message and know I would have my chance to make it back home. As I learned of the Atonement, I had hope—real hope for the first time—that I could be forgiven for what seemed like a long string of bad decisions.

My life has been full of challenges. But I choose to grasp all I can to assure my passage back to my Heavenly Father. I am thankful that I was found and brought into the fold. May God bless everyone looking to find Him.

Linda Collins is the mother of two and grandmother of two. She is grateful she did not listen to the doctors the day her daughter was born but, instead, insisted on picking up and holding her baby. The baby's health gradually improved; she stopped having seizures by age five but continued to have challenges with her legs due to cerebral palsy. Today this wonderful daughter's oldest son is serving in the mission field. Linda's second daughter has also grown into a wonderful young woman and works for a university as a nurse educator. Linda says that joining the Church has brought many blessings to their family. She continues to study the scriptures daily. "I'm filled with contentment and assurance that I'm on the right path and that the Lord is aware of me."

Yea, they shall not be beaten down by the storm at the last day; yea, neither shall they be harrowed up by the whirlwinds; but when the storm cometh they shall be gathered together in their place, that the storm cannot penetrate to them.

—Alma 26:6

$\mathscr{A}$ WINDY
WEDDING DAY TALE

By Sara Hacken

My daughter's much-anticipated wedding took place in June 1992. We had the day all planned out. First, we would drive to the Manti Utah Temple, where she was to be married. Then we'd drive the two-plus hours back to Orem, Utah, where we planned to meet at a park for a bridal luncheon, and finally, we'd hold a small reception at our home. It was a wedding on a budget, and we were happy to help make it memorable. As it turned out, her wedding day became memorable, all right, but for another reason.

Since I was a single, working mom on a limited budget, I felt the entire responsibility of getting everything ready. The details seemed overwhelming. We sewed layered tablecloths, made our own flower arrangements, and worked hard sewing dresses for all of my daughter's sisters and bridesmaids. My daughter asked a friend to draw a pencil sketch of her with her fiancé, and we used it to make invitations. It was both unique and inexpensive.

When my daughter said she wanted her wedding reception in our tiny backyard, I was surprised. It wasn't carefully groomed and landscaped, but with some work, it would do. So we set to work buying new shrubs, trimming edges, planting flowers, killing weeds in the ditch alongside our house, planting our vegetable garden, and mending the wood fence. It was rewarding to see things start to take shape.

My mother helped buy the wedding dress. I made a hat with a veil on it, and with a few more purchases of a wedding book, feathered pen, and jewelry, we were ready.

At the end of the semester, the kids arrived home just in time to put the finishing touches on the festivities. We ordered a six-foot-long sub sandwich for the picnic bridal luncheon, and for the reception, we prepared mounds of grapes and made trays of baklava, homemade mints, and mixed nuts. One of her friends offered to make the wedding cake. It wasn't fancy, but we had fun baking and preparing the food together.

Finally, the big day arrived—complete with heavy clouds and lots of wind. I tried not to worry about it. Many family members drove to the Manti Temple, and most of us got there on time. The ceremony was perfect, and we were thrilled that so many of the family attended. But as we drove back to Orem, the sky darkened, and the wind picked up. We arrived at the park and began setting paper plates and the sandwich out on picnic tables, but the wind whipped everything away faster than we could anchor it all. Within minutes, the sandwiches and drinks had blown into our laps or across the grass and were piling up against a chain-link fence. I already felt a little embarrassed because I could only afford a simple picnic instead of a nice restaurant meal, but even that suddenly became a disaster. We rescued what we could, held on to *everything*, and ate quickly.

A short time later, we packed up and drove to my house to get things ready for the reception. We had put my daughter's beautiful hat/veil in the back of the van to keep it from blowing away, but when we arrived home, we discovered that red punch had spilled all over it. First the lunch had all but blown away and now another small disaster. What else could happen?

As the time for the reception drew near, I put the veil in to soak, then set out the tablecloths and decorations on the tables. By this time, the wind had worsened, if that was possible, and as quickly as we set out our lovely centerpieces, they were whisked away and tumbled across the grass. Our beautiful tablecloths went flying, and it became disaster number three.

This was my sweet daughter's wedding, and as all mothers did, I had worked *hard* to make it special with what little means I had. I hurt inside as I saw everything getting wrecked. I had done the best I could to make the day special, and now all my hard work was getting carried off by this unusually fierce wind. I wanted to cry.

About thirty minutes before the reception began, we all met in our tiny living room. What should we do? We clearly couldn't hold an outdoor reception with the stormy, windy weather blowing everything away and only getting worse by the minute.

At that point, my mother suggested we pray. I agreed and asked if she would lead us in our petition. With faith born of long experience, she prayed that the elements would be tempered so we could hold the reception. She prayed for peace in our little yard and that the wind would not disturb anything until the reception ended. She prayed that all of us would enjoy the occasion and asked that it be made a success.

And then we all went out into the backyard to set everything in place. It was perfectly quiet and calm. Not even the edge of a tablecloth moved, because there wasn't any wind. Right at six thirty, people started to come. They mingled, ate, and congratulated the newlyweds.

About halfway through the reception, one of our good ward members arrived and said, "I didn't know if you'd even be having a reception, but I decided to drop by anyway. I've just come from the Little League fields in town, and they have cancelled all of the games because of the wind. Your yard must be kind of sheltered because there's no wind here at all. I'm really surprised."

We knew better. It was the power of prayer from an inspired and concerned grandma.

It was a lovely reception until the wind suddenly started blowing again. Decorations flew off the tables, food scattered to the ground, the lovingly stitched wedding quilt fell over, and people ran for cover.

Everyone quickly mobilized to chase down the decorations, bring in the food, and rescue the quilt. It was the fastest wedding clean-up I'd ever seen. Then we looked at the clock. The storm hit our yard at almost exactly eight thirty, the time the reception had been scheduled to end. As we realized my mom's prayer had been answered exactly as she had asked, we looked at each other in wonder. We were humbled to realize that a loving Heavenly Father cared enough about one family's wedding that the elements were tempered for us that day.

Sara Hacken is the Young Women president in her ward, and she has also served as a Sunday School teacher, a Relief Society president, a seminary teacher, and a Boy Scout merit badge counselor. She loves teaching history to junior high school students, and she dresses up to do colonial reenactments during summer holidays. Sara is the mother of four children and the grandmother of thirteen grandchildren.

I can do all things through Christ which strengtheneth me.

—Philippians 4:13

How BLESSED AM I
By Beth Shumway Moore

Pain from one of my toes radiated throughout my foot, making it impossible for most of my shoes to fit comfortably. The pain continued to worsen to the point that walking became extremely difficult. My middle toe turned a bright red, and whenever the doctor pressed on it, the area around it hurt worse. He was baffled over what the problem might be.

To complicate the problem, arthritis had crippled my toes, making it difficult to completely locate the source of the pain. The doctor suggested surgery to straighten the toes and help him locate the problem. I agreed.

My family lived some distance away, and, though it seems strange looking back on it now, I didn't inform them about what was happening to me. I really didn't think it could be too serious. A friend drove me to the hospital so I could have the surgery on a Thursday and later, after the surgery, brought me home. Friday night when the doctor called to check on me, I indicated that things seemed fine. I didn't mention that my foot hurt when I stepped on it. Of course some pain would still linger after surgery, I reasoned. Plus, I was taking pain medications.

Two of my stalwart neighbors gave me a priesthood blessing, and I slept well that night. Saturday should have been a much better day, yet I felt something was wrong. I shared my uneasy feelings with the doctor, and he suggested I try several things. He was, and is, a very efficient doctor, but he didn't think my problem was serious. However, I became increasingly concerned. Without my having to ask, my friends gave me another healing blessing, and I never doubted I would recover.

My continued distress must have been obvious because that night my friend and neighbor worried about leaving me alone. I assured her I was fine, and she left.

I slept well until around 3:00 a.m., when I woke up confused and filled with pain. I felt convinced I was dying! Desperately praying, I felt inspired through the haze of my pain- and drug-filled body to get up and call 911, then unlock the door, get my purse, and lie back down. I did and felt relieved, assured that help was on the way. Luck or answer to prayer? I knew the answer to that.

The ambulance was in the area and came quickly. In the short time I'd been waiting, my strength had failed, and I couldn't even raise my head. The two medics had to lift me onto a stretcher and put IVs in my arms before they carried me out to the ambulance. Sirens roared as I was taken to the emergency room. I remember being vaguely aware of men and women dressed in white surrounding me, but I knew it wasn't heaven because heaven couldn't smell like the emergency area. More needles were put in my arms, and after about six hours, I became more alert. I could ask and answer questions, though when an aide called my friend to come for me, I didn't even know where I was.

Once home, after large doses of medication and whatever else they'd given me, I slept through the rest of the day and the night. Upon awakening around 8:00 a.m., I called my doctor immediately, and he told me to come in before his regular patients arrived. Again a friend came and picked me up to take me in.

Upon seeing my foot, the doctor immediately began treatment, and he continued working on my foot for about an hour every morning for two weeks. Only later when I was well on the road to recovery did he tell me he had been horrified at the sight that met his eyes that day: most of the flesh had been eaten off my toes. I'd caught the feared and dreaded MRSA, a fast, flesh-eating bacteria. He feared he'd never save my toes, so he worked hard in the hope he could at least save my foot.

Later I found out that he had wanted me in the hospital, but he was afraid in my weakened state I might contract other germs and possibly spread mine. So with devoted friends helping and regular priesthood blessings, I recovered, never realizing the worry and fear of those around me. Somehow I never doubted I'd be healed. The doctor later admitted that he didn't have a good night's sleep for the two weeks he worked on me. Two nurses said how blessed I was that he'd spent the time to try to cure me because they thought some doctors would have cut off the toes before it spread further. That would have been the quick remedy. But this dear man took the time to save my foot, my toes, and maybe more.

Never again did I take walking for granted. I'm especially grateful that, at the age of eighty-six, I can still take care of myself. The pain I endured before the surgery never returned.

Life can change quickly, and mine would have changed drastically if I'd lost a foot. Gratitude fills my heart.

My Heavenly Father and His Son, Jesus Christ, have blessed me so abundantly. I feel so fortunate to belong to the restored Church, where inspired priesthood blessings can bring about miracles. I pray that I can fulfill the promises I made in the premortal existence: to endure to the end and be worthy to live with my loved ones again . . . in the relatively near future.

Beth Shumway Moore, eighty-six, survived her rural childhood in Lovell, Wyoming, and moved shortly after high school graduation to Utah. After earning her bachelor and master's degrees, she taught elementary school for thirty-two years. Beth has won many awards for articles, stories, and essays and has published two historical novels. She was honored by the League of Utah Writers in 2009 as Writer of the Year. Today she spends much of her time with her children and grandchildren, and she says they are the frosting on the cake of her life.

Whosoever shall put their trust in God shall be supported in their trials, and their troubles, and their afflictions, and shall be lifted up at the last day.

—*Alma 36:3*

WAS MY WORK GOOD ENOUGH?
By Carolyn Campbell

I was a stringer, or local reporter, for a major news magazine. I had completed several small assignments for this publication when an important story broke in Salt Lake City and the stringer who was usually first choice was out of town for a week of vacation. The magazine assigned the story to me, but just in case I didn't write it to their satisfaction, they also flew in a staff reporter from Los Angeles.

When he arrived, I had already started interviewing sources and writing the story. He was friendly and encouraging. He said I had made a good start, but I was also impressed with how he jumped into the story himself, found additional sources, and completed many additional interviews quickly. I was both worried and intimidated. What would happen to me if my story didn't meet the editors' satisfaction? If they had planned to fly someone in from out of state, why had they assigned the story to me? What would it mean to my future if my work was considered substandard?

The story was about a well-known murder case. The parents of the murdered woman were divorced, and when I met with the father for our scheduled interview, he thought his daughter was still considered missing. After I asked a question or two, I realized he hadn't been told that she had been found. I had a decision to make. Was I more concerned about breaking the news and watching his immediate reaction for the sake of my article, or should I let family members tell him privately? I decided it wasn't my place to break that news. I then had to journalistically shift gears and interview him while trying not to give a single hint that I knew the girl had been found dead. When he said, "I am going to keep hoping," my heart went out to him. I listened as he shared happy memories of the daughter he loved and hoped would be found alive.

How to write the article in the face of so many strong emotions became a challenge. Feeling both competitive and unsure of myself, I started to try to follow in this other reporter's footsteps. If I could somehow absorb his technique and write the story in a manner similar to his, I was sure it would be excellent. I worked hard, but I became increasingly discouraged and unsure of myself, my instincts, and my abilities.

One morning when I was particularly exhausted, when I thought I couldn't stretch myself any further to try to reach a goal I wasn't even sure I was nearing, I paused. Suddenly, I felt an invisible presence wrap an arm around my shoulder. The feeling was as clear and definite as if I could feel an actual person standing beside me. The unseen arm wrapped me in a comforting, reassuring hug. There were no words but only the strongly distinct feeling that I should write the story in the way that felt right to me and not try to copy the other reporter's technique.

I sat down and began writing the story in my own way, using my own instincts and the skills that had carried me through thirty years as a freelance writer. When I finished the story, I reluctantly submitted it online and waited. A few hours later, the out-of-town reporter called me. My heart thudded when I saw his number on my caller ID. What was he about to tell me? By now, I was completely exhausted and wondering if I had taken the wrong path. After I said hello, he said, "That draft you submitted was perfect. You should be very proud of yourself."

At his kind words, tears fell.

Then he continued. "I liked how you really made it your own."

The next day the national editor-in chief phoned me.

"You have done an amazing job on the story," he said. "You are the talk of New York."

I can't imagine anyone ever saying that to me again, but in the moment I replied that I very much appreciated receiving the assignment.

"Just bask in how wonderful you are."

A few weeks later a bonus check for several hundred dollars arrived in my mailbox.

I have never regretted my decision to respect that father's grief. And I will never forget the feeling of an arm around my shoulder in a moment when I doubted myself. I will always be grateful for the help I received. Now during discouraging and uncertain times, I recall that moment and am able to summon the courage to go on, despite what life hands me.

After this experience, I wrote many other stories for the magazine. I never felt feelings of hesitation or doubt again in working with the editors and staff. I grew to know some of them personally, and memories of working with them are among my fondest recollections.

Carolyn Campbell is the mother of four and the author of three books and more than 800 magazine articles.

In the heav'ns are parents single?
No, the thought makes reason stare!
Truth is reason; truth eternal
Tells me I've a mother there.

—*"O My Father,"* Hymns, *no. 292*

MOTHER'S LOVE
Name Withheld

I was saying my prayer, thanking Heavenly Father for my countless blessings and His watchful care, when the thought occurred to me that although we rightly thank Heavenly Father for everything, we also have a Heavenly Mother who quietly stays in the background. We never think or talk about Her, but She taught us as spirit children, She tended and watched over us, and She loved us.

I added to my prayer a thank you for Her kindness and love. And then into my mind came this sweet, gentle woman's voice: *I love you too.*

I wanted to end this collection of stories with that sweet reminder of "Mother's Love." We are all part of an eternal family, and we are most assuredly deeply loved and watched over by heavenly parents and angels who are authorized to give us help and comfort under the direction of our Lord Jesus Christ.

If you would like to comment on any of these stories or send a message to an author, you may send an e-mail to judyedits@gmail.com, and I will be sure to get your comments to the right person.

ABOUT THE AUTHOR

Judy C. Olsen has been writing and editing for LDS audiences for many years. She graduated from BYU in child development and family relations, then went to work for a year before she met and married Donald L. Olsen. Their family lived in Las Vegas for nearly twenty years.

Judy began writing freelance for Church magazines and other publications while raising her family in Nevada. She also served on the public affairs committee for the Southern Nevada area and helped with publicity for the Las Vegas Temple dedication and open house.

When her family moved to Utah, she returned to the workplace, where she spent five years as the family editor for the *Ensign* magazine, among other assignments. Her work appears in all four Church magazines: *Liahona*, *Ensign*, *New Era*, and *Friend*.

Judy served a mission to North Argentina in her youth and later with Don in the Utah Salt Lake South Mission, where she and her husband served as part-time missionaries assisting the elders in the Hispanic community.

The Olsens are the parents of four children and the grandparents of eighteen grandchildren.